PAY THE PRICE

…until you have you can never be!!!

Ezeh, Thomas Chinedu

Copyright © 2020 Pay the price

All rights reserved

The characters and events portrayed in this book are fictitious. Any similarity to real persons, living or dead, is coincidental and not intended by the author.

No part of this book may be reproduced, or stored in a retrieval system, or transmitted in any form or by any means, electronic, mechanical, photocopying, recording, or otherwise, without express written permission of the publisher.

ISBN: 9798697069608

Cover design by:
Library of Congress Control Number:
Printed in the United States of America

I dedicate this microscopic work of determination to the almighty God, God of all flesh and those that have decided to be Determined.

Foreword

Yes many are in the street of success, many are yet to discover the street, some have been deceived that it is their destiny to succeed while most people have been threatened that aside determination, there can never be success; yet they do not know DETERMINATION.

How then can I succeed, they enquire? Wonder no more, for right in your hand is Mr. Determination. Follow it diligently, gently and you will be glad you did.

Don't forget

...the presence of falls and failing along your paths, is an assurance of victory if only you can press on. My problem has been why will I fail or why did i fail - the issue is not failed but what caused your failure.

This work has considered some rudiments of achieving success - as has been exhibited by men of valor who have made their impress in world record.

it's a book that will broaden your heart on: Deciding, Executing, Targeting, Evaluating, Resisting, Motivating, Identifying, Navigating, Achieving, Terminating, Illuminating and ordering for Opportunities within Necessities.

It promises to be thrilling,!!!

for comments, criticisms and motivational talks,
send me a mail at etcgrp85@gmail.com or call +234(0)809 047 8999.

Introduction

In a way of introduction, I want to officially welcome you to this microscopic element of work a stratum for provoking desire to achieve, termed; DETERMINATION.

I refer this work as microscopic element because of inability of people to feel the important role of "determination" i.e. achieving success. Moreover, if you will agree with these; it is only microscopic things that rule and shake the world think about Uranium 235 and micro-organisms.

My candid advice to you is to bury all you know previously and pay rasp attention to this expository and inspirational minded work of philosophy. Remember "the world is too busy to wait for you, so, you better learn how to wait for the world". By giving your maximum attention to this work I can assure you that you will get something that will help you wait for the ever busy and dynamic world of ours- stay pined and glued to the pages.

Hey! Dear!! you are here !!!

I am pleased to welcome you to the point of DETERMINATION, are you ready?

… Let go there!!! It's a dogma of determination.

Preface

To every life goal, objective and dream, there is a "PRICE" No matter how small or big the dream might be, there is always a "PRICE TO PAY". The magnitude of the price to be paid is inversely and directly proportional to your dream. But at every state of equilibrium, the ultimate price required of every dream - irrespective of any other factor affecting the dream is "DETERMINATION" which has been broadly explained as a DOGMA in this piece of work tagged; PAY THE PRICE. It is a widely accepted fact, that the only price aside the "God Father" paid by the achieved, the successful and the creme de la creme of the society is "Determination".

Being good or bad is a choice, but there is always an ultimate price that can posit you to achieving whichever one, you have chosen for yourself. But achieving Whatever you desire, thought of or dream of; you must be ready and willing to "PAT THE PRICE" through determination as inscribed in this work.

This book will teach you how to acquire this skills with in depth understanding of - the do's and Don't in "paying the price"

◆ ◆ ◆

Do not forget!!
   ...the cashless price of achievement is Determination !!!
         Please, pay the Price

◆ ◆ ◆

APPROBATIONS

The author of this work, Chinedu, relentlessly demanded that I glance through it and write something about the work. When eventually despite my tight schedules I flipped through the book, I said to myself:

"This work ought to be read by every young person of our time"

In the present day society when things appear to be in a state of topsy-forydom, when the global economic crises looks like a cloud hovering over the future of young people, this book comes as a great source of encouragement, in business, in family life and even in search of faith. The author has used his personal experience to make his point vivid. I sincerely encourage everyone but in a very special way, the young people-graduates, undergraduates, new couples etc to take hold of the message this book brings across to their world.

Determination remains the only key to success. However, let us not fail to be determined about our ultimate goal, which is the salvation of our souls.

Once more, I congratulate the author for his determination in this work and i recommend it for all determined and yet to be determined people.

Rev. Fr. Dr. Lawerence O. I Iwuamadi (Ssl, Phd)
Chaplain: St. Thomas Aquinas Catholic Chaplaincy,
Federal University of Technology, Owerri,
Imo State, Nigeria.

TABLE OF CONTENT
- Introduction
- Definition / Meaning
- Just What You Need
- Numeracy of Determination
- Oddity of Determination
- Litany of Determination
- Repetition in Determination
- Philosophy of Determination
- Rudiments of Determination
- What Does It Mean to Be Determined?
- The Greatest Prison of The World
- True Test for Determination Is Difficulties
- Pathway of Determination

- My Journey into The Path of Determination
- Analogy of Achievement & Determination
- Determination the Only Catalyst for Achievement
- Scientific Proof of Determination

Hey! Dear!!

you are here!!!

I am pleased to welcome you to the point of DETERMINATION, are you ready?
...Let go there!!!

It's a dogma of determination.

◆ ◆ ◆

What a fascination?

Since my several years and decades of earthly sojourn, I have wondered and pondered on various issues pertaining to humanity. Continually, I have worried why the continuous and endless struggle in the life of human race? What is the cause of insatiability in humanity and perpetual search in life? Even when Christianity preaches that life is vanity and all in it is vanity but it does not deter man for once! Not even propagators of Christianity. In my quest for response to these lives pricking questions and the authenticity of the spiritual quotation-"vanity upon vanity all is vanity". I decided to follow up an event that happened in the University of Technology Owerri. One certain year, there erupted communal crisis between the students and host communities of the University "Futo-Oziobodo Crisis" where a life of struggle was wasted and a final year project student of 1st class status was lost, in bitterness I vowed to see the last of him, so followed the union down to the mortuary. On getting there, we demanded to see the remain of our fellow comrade, unfortunately for us the young man was not yet embalmed he (it) was just dumped where other corpse yet to be attended to were "so, friends", the Mortician said "only those that has mind should enter" I Mr. maturity batched in as number three (3) on getting there I saw the whole man of yesterday, a struggler and a hussar of yesterday lying helpless like a log of wood without a single thing on him "naked they were in there" there and then I agreed that vanity upon vanity all is vanity and so my thought was once again greatly triggered, what is our mission on earth? Why all these restlessness?

The truth sad story is that everybody is involved these is no exception, immediately I was recalled with the union motivational slogan……off the greatest Nigerian student, great……. Aluta continua!! Victoria ascerta!!! Meaning; struggle continues!! Victory is assured" it became obviously clear to me that the struggle of life is geared towards "achievement" be it victory, call it success or greatness all is aiming towards "**ACHIEVING**"

I realized that man was destined to be in great search to "achieving" in life until the world of vanity comes. Pause a minute! Is life all about achievement", please do not continue until you have an answer to this question. Stick to your answer does not change it but do, once you have gone through the pages of this book. It is a de-facto that life is all about achievement. Dear Thomas, what do you think, Prof. what about you?

Take a close consideration to these, Lucifer, Satan was an angel of God, thrown down to earth out of his looming desire to achieve what? Equality with God agreed! Not yet convinced okay it was

Satan, what about Eve and Adam? Eve fell for sin because of her yearning desire to achieve – what – knowledge of what is good and bad.

Dear friend do not misunderstand me, achievement is not something bad nor evil, after all it was in the beat for achievement that you and I was created "let us make man in our own image" we were even commissioned to achieve whatever we want to achieve – go into the world flourish and multiply".

So do not miss the point I am only trying to let you know that life is all about achievement. There is one unknown fact of the world – Everybody is mandated to achieve, in fact you are commissioned on earth to achieve get it into your skull if you do not achieve, you are liable to damnation and dejection at all point.

It is on account of this that every soul, young and Old, children, youth, parent, mothers and fathers all live to achieve, many will rather live to achieve than achieving just existence for in achieving we can live. Others on the other hand will rather prefer to achieve to live or even die achieving rather than not achieving at all. Whichever you agree with the fact is what life is all about achievement.

Whether you believe in achievement or not is not the case here, but the fact that the achieved are respected and admired makes it an attractive thing. No matter what you do, the underlying motive is nothing else than to achieve.

If you doubt this why are you reading this book? Beloved, the best thing you will do for yourself this year is to read this microscopic element with full acceptance of its philosophy because they are divinely inspirited, it is not written for that which you gave out before you received it but rather that the marvelous work of the creator will be awaken in you and the surest way to achieving anything in life shown to you because - you can never be until you are.

Meaning that, that which you want to achieve in life can never be achieved until you are determined. And you ca never be determined until you understand what it means to be determined. I have decided to share this divine direction gotten from God because it is not mine though came through me it's not meant for me but for the world. The idea of this microscopic element came unto me several times at different occasion at different hour and the Trinity Sunday mandated me to put it down (19/06/2011) Abuja.

I have toured through the pages of several success story books, great motivational speakers achievement stories and biography of so many successful and achieved in the society and the authors of these write-ups have been able to convey nothing into my brain rather than a 13 letter word named **Determination;** that was not enough for me, it still was unable to get me to where I am going to, because majority of them end up leaving me in the middle of the sea, as they will withhold what "determination is and how to be determined.

I know that you can never give this kind of story after going through this book I can assure you I have done that which they couldn't do by the help of the Holy Spirit.

Hey!! let get started - don't get tired lazy chap.

don't forget!!!
….."The world is too busy to wait for you – so you better learn how to

wait for the world".

I am off to the next junction join me as I leap - Look !!!

Wait a minute!

What do you understand as **ACHIEVEMENT?** – for me it is a word or world buried in determination" are you serious I don't know!! But that is what I think what about you? I know I am not too wrong because most of the authors of all the books I have read on achievement, success and greatness, place determination as the surest way to achieving success or victory let see what the dictionary has to say about this; According to Oxford advanced Leaner's, *the word achievement was defined as "a thing that somebody has done successfully, especially using their own EFFORT AND SKILL" it also has it as the act or process of achieving something.* It went further to state that a small success gives *A SENSE OF ACHIEVEMEMNT* i.e. achievement can be felt, if you have achieved, you will know and people around you must know as they will feel your heat and air, you may be wondering why I capitalized the word EFFORT and skill nothing more but an indication that achievement demands your effort and skill so it is a product of your hard effort and skills. In reality what does it mean to achieve? How do people know or one know that he or she has achieved. I would not be surprise if you doubt the fact that people achieve everyday without knowing that they are achieving while other pray to achieve without achieving. So what does it mean to achieve? It means to succeed in reaching a particular Goal, TARGET, status or standard, especially by making an "effort" for a Long time i.e. victory in doing or causing something to happen – the same Oxford dictionary calls it *ACCOMPLISH".*

From the above definition, it's obviously clear that you cannot talk of achievement, success or accomplishment without a Goal / Targets. And **Target or Goal are only but illusion, if you do not decide to channel your effort and skill towards it,** when I talk of decision I don't mean easier said than done decision but do or die, good or bad kind of decision.

If you are following semantically, you will see the reason for most author of motivational and inspiration books tying the key to achievement, success with determination. And you will not hesitate in concurring with my earlier statement that - achievement is a word/world buried in Determination.

In other words, **to be determined is to consistently and vigorously work for that achievement buried in the world of determination over a long time.** Hello dear, the word sounds so easy to be pronounced but, too heavy to carry to comprehension. "Is somebody with me or have you lost track or dosed off? Wake!! We just started.

Now **don't forget – you are too microscopic for the world to remember but microscopic things rules and hold the world"** You and I are aware of microchips and microwaves aren't we? Yes we are! Let's ride on.

You are holding this book for a purpose, once you accomplish drop it do not read further.

...microscopic elements! Microscopic you!!! And microscopic world!!!

Hello!

Is somebody still carried along?

I am glad to know that you are coming behind the biro! To stimulate your appetite let me welcome you to just what you need to achieve.

JUST WHAT YOU NEED

Beloved we unanimously agreed that determination swallowed achievement and your quest to find the word in the world is the desire to achieve didn't we? Okay! Even if you do not agree with me, from your previous text you did agree with authors that the only secret of achieving anything in life is determination, not so? If you are not in agreement with it, I shall try my best here to giving it some scientific analysis, just be calm and watch me as I imbibe numeracy into what I call **NUMEROLOGY OF DETERMINATION.**

Meanwhile let understand the psychology of determination. It is a very lengthy word that discourages on sight and pain striking in pronouncing, though sweet at the ear when successfully pronounced. It was derived from the head word determine but mean different thing though might be similar a times. Its meaning is as discouraging as its length.

Unfortunately you! As success conscious soul can't do without it. My lexicon defined it as; *the quality that makes you continues to do something even when this is difficult!*

That one is a comprehensive program to me; all it conveyed to me is that determination is an enduring quality for difficulties – i.e. difficulty is the only test for determination!! This did not meet my definition for determination, I do not know about you. A second look at it in the same dictionary defined it as **the process of deciding something officially** and both quantified it as an uncountable noun.

Like we all learnt, a noun is defined as a name of an object, animal's places or things – so where is determination? If I can still recollect it should be an abstract noun, that means you can only feel determined but can never see nor touch it, it implies that you have holistic right to define it the way it would suit you.

The two definition above before you can't get what is required of you to ACHIEVE anything on earth; a merge of the two may to some extent help you. You might have had people say you are not serious!

Mostly young ladies use it on their admirers when they feel that the zeal is not in them or that the guys could not meet up with their demand, and most a times that often triggers their determination to be serious.

And so, goes to any length to gaining the ladies attention Determination demands for certain characters either to be acquired or inherited. Some of these characters could be in the definition earlier provided.

Characteristics such as Endurance, Persistence, decision and target were exposed in the above definition as time goes on we shall elaborate on the other intricate quality demanded by determination.

I hope you are catching the joke of the century sequentially! Okay let ride on!!!

If you are already aware of the previous pages not next pages.

NUMERACY OF DETERMINATION

It important to note that no knowledge is wasted, stay focused as I use number to explain the efficacy of determination in your quest for achievements. Taking a count of the letters of determination you will see that it contain (13) letters, it has four of its letter repeated two (2) or three (3) times and each letters of the alphabet has numbers attached to them. We shall sum up these number assigned to the alphabet so as to make reference to magnitude / direction, position etc, Watch it live:

- D → 4
- E → 5
- T → 20
- E → 5
- R → 18
- M → 13
- I → 9
- N → 14

- A → 1
- T → 20
- I → 9
- O → 15
- 13   N → 14
      147%

Like I noticed earlier there is something odd and repeating about the word determination. It will be absurd if you are confused at this point, just follow the ink as the biro print.

ODDITY OF DETERMINATION

It is very unusual with the numbers found within this thirteen (13) lettered word odd number. If you sum the numbers assigned to the alphabet you must get an odd number. From my little knowledge of odd numbers they are only divisible by one and itself.

It implies that determination is a sole individual, personal responsibility. Even if it is a group thing, there must still be one man who shoulders that determination.

Have you ever encountered an even numbered committee in a democratic setting?

It's alway odd for that determination power of achieving success / victory, to buttress my point in the cardinality of the assigned numbers of the alphabet is still, a single one (1) standing at a very far end of the word at position (9) nine a very unique and unreal number too, that is divisible by 1, 3, and 9 it is odd too.

Imperatively no one can influence your determination.
You can never be forced to be determined, in other words;

father, mother, brother, sister can only advice you to be deter-

mined but it is a thing of the mind and the mind is solely owned and controlled by you.

Y es you the one reading this microscopic element of work. Determination is a mysterious thing once you take it, all your engagement will result in mysterious achievement. If you doubt me, consult suicide bombers, inventors and scientist.

The Dogma of determination is too clear for anyone to contest, *only the dogmatic wear the sackcloth of determination and only the determined achieve in this world of dynamic and jettison world of ours.*

I will not be happy if you move through the pages of this book without getting the subject matter, it is going to be a wasted effort on my own side. I can't imagine myself seating for hours just to fables. I am not writing this because I am less busy, but because I want you to have an indent understanding of what determination is all about.

You know, each time we see the achieved celebrated and we are opportune to talk with them the 1st question we often ask is; what is the secrete and two things remains the answer, my brother, my sister – Na God oh, but I serve God too?

And the next answer will be and Determination you will foolishly nod your empty head and zoom away without asking him or her-what determination means and how he was determined. *Pretending to know why we don't – killer of the proud.*

Thank God you are reading this microscopic element of work,

read it with your soul ok!

Don't forget
...we are in a strange world where strange things happen alongside with odd things so get odd, get determined for you to happen!
Come on with me as we naked determination!!!

◆ ◆ ◆

LITANY OF DETERMINATION

As earlier explained the word is too boring to pronounce, but sweet at the end of the pronunciation. Of the thirteen letters that made up the word, only five (5) is not repeated the other letters were repeated twice (2ce). I have the conviction to tell you to note that feature. Five (5) single letters (odd number) and four (4) repeated letter (remember number 4 started the word determination) i.e. without repetition, nine (9) letters in characters were rearranged to form the word.

We have earlier stated the uniqueness of the digit (9) a symbolic number that ends the unity numbers in numeracy, also if you find the median of the word determination it is (9) nine, see you just have to believe the uniqueness of this word determination imperatively, **to have determination is to have expected end of being at the peak.** Recall that unit numbers indicate completeness, agreement, being single. It from these unit number that every other numbers are formed as earlier established, no matter how you re-arrange the assigned numbers of the letters in the word determination you must still arrive at odd number.

Watch this!!

If you sum up this nine none repeated letters, you will get ninety nine 99 an odd number. It implies that if all things being equal with determination you are ninety nine (99%) sure of achieving success and in every shortcoming or failing have at least 48% success in it.

Now let me tell you why most of the letters were repeated.

REPETITION IN DETERMINATION

The letters were repeated to inform you that in the world of determination you cannot do away with trials and retrial i.e. there must always be a first time and that means determination is not seen in 1st attempt but in 2nd attempt, more so, that there will always be room to retry but trying to make it at 1st trial will keep you ahead of others.

It also implies that succeeding at a second trial makes you far and better than the person that tried just once – check it out by the time you repeat the four values in determination you will have 13 while in your 1st trial you had only 9 – it give you a better experience with deeper understanding.

Don't forget……adversities make a genius while prosperity conceals it general philosophy

Hey friends!

Are we still together?

I guess you are getting tired! So am I, but can't help it than to obey my thought and write as it forces me to.

For you, I suggest you stop and sip a glass of water and join us again, what about that?

Or is this guy saying jargons and repeating what you already know?

Oh sorry !!!

I am not perfect but remember;
of all you know, it is not up to one tenth of the reality – so why boost.

And

that the greatest weapon of self destruction is assumption of literacy in web of your ignorance.

Also

he who does not know and does not know that he does not know is not only a fool but can never know.

Finally, if you must continue, take a very good note of these;

…there are so many things you don't know some you can never know, you must not know them. Don't even bother to know them but you must believe in them.

I have sounded this for those who will like to know and understand all the philosophies of this dogma of determination to take note.

PHILOSOPHY OF DETERMINATION

I shall philosophize-determination without an alteration to my divine inspirations as;
the ability to decide on an evaluated target, executing it without regret to your motivating identity or Ideas nor negotiating with your achievement plans and tactically terminating all obstacles illuminated while ordering for opportunities in all necessities.
Yes!
That is my philosophy on determination it involve my all and I put in my all once I want to talk about it. I see determination as a code i.e. an

acronyms for the required rudimental qualities and characteristics for being that which you want to be.

And I firmly believe that you can never be that, that you hunger for until you are determined. Join me as I decode the hidden qualities of greatness swallowed by determination.

Watch it life and direct do not be told;

D	DECISION
E	EVALUATION
T	TARGET
E	EXECUTION
R	RESISTANCE / REGRET
M	MOTIVATION
I	IDENTITY / IDEALISM
N	NO NEGOTIATION, NO NEGATIVITY
A	*'achievement'*
T	TEMINATION
I	ILLUMINATION
O	ORDER FOR OPPOTUNITY
N	NECESSITIES

Surprise! Aren't you? Well! Don't be, we are just getting started. You may wonder how these words came about; wonder no more it is one of those divine inspirational gifts from God. Just read it by the time you are done you must believe in them. The fact remains that you can never touch any of the hidden factors for achievement without making reference to the other if actually you are on the right track. You can never understand it until I debug it.

I do not know if you noticed something about that scaring word? Did you see that which it swallowed? I told you earlier on that we needed to perform a surgery on determination to bring out that which makes life very restless and to be in continuous struggle.

Take a close look at those words listed; can you see that tiny word achievement? It is standing at position nine (9) again and it started with letter A having figure 1 odd number again and we unanimously agreed that the number 1 cause of life struggle is **ACHIEVEMENTS**. Just relax I shall pick and expose each of those unique qualities demanded by achievement for potential **achievers.**

...you have seen nothing yet...just stay glued to your chair as we unravel the mystery.

Hello friend! Nice to know you are here!!!.
Have you not read enough relax now!

Your money has almost expires and the ink is still running. who told you that the ink is running because of your cash!! Never!!!

Beloved, with heavy heart of determination and great reference to your quest for achievement I have the singular honor to invite and at the same time welcome you too to...

RUDIMENTS OF DETERMINATION

In my little world of Adventure and Adversities, I have not seen neither have I heard of any one that make do of anything without concrete reference to the 1st acronym on the world and the word determination.

In fact, it is a very important quality that should be possessed by all but a lot of people lacks it a great deal. You know what I am talking about its nothing else but Mr. D

DECISION

Unfortunately it starts the end of man death, though life & death is a choice.

...Listen, die if you must, provided it is the will of your decision.
If you have ever made decision then you will agree with me that it is the most difficult things on earth yes or yes? Have a flash back on our numeracy of determination it was (4) four, meaning that it allows for opinions.

It implies there will be multiple options while making a decision. Are you aware that no matter how many opinion you may sort that 95% of it is still your responsibility recall that in numeracy the nine none-repeated letters gave 99% assurance of success once you are determined take decision into consideration you still have 95 part to play in your life decision. Even life itself is all about deciding - choice, the Christian Scripture say I present to you, LIFE and Death choose one – Decision. It went further to suggest that you choose life.

Wait a second!

Can you mention anything in life, anything at all that does not involve decision or choice making? Decision making is of different levels and degrees but the one of reference here is painstaking, life making, and acute Decision.

The dictionary will say it is **"a choice or judgment that you make after thinking and talking about what is the best thing to do"** that is in its own mind - what do you think?

To me this is not the decision that leads to determination. Before you can say I have made a decision you must make reference to other rudiment of determination.

I define decision as **taking a stand on a target and standing by it until you are six feet (6'ft') below the street of achievement or six feet above the globe of success, victory over trials. Please note that** *you have a decision made only when you are ready to die for your decision i.e. getting prepared to suffer or gain from your choice. – Simply put, dumping yourself to the will of your decision.*

I was listening to met fm on one faithful Sunday it was reported that a Norwegian has accepted responsibility in Oslo for attempting a massacre in a youth camp which claimed number of lives and left many injured when asked he said the act was quite awful but necessary, that he shall see them in court where he was charged for act of terrorism. This is exactly what it means to take a decision; he is ready to stand by his decision. His response showed no sign of regrets to his execution though painful.

◆ ◆ ◆

WHAT DOES IT MEANS TO DECIDE?

You have not decided: as in, there is no decision yet if there is no forensic <u>evaluation</u> of all available options. Remember <u>Evaluation</u> is still one of the rudiments of determination. Hear this, there is no decision on this earth and there will never be any one without a <u>target,</u> yes I mean "target" – every life target have a <u>motivating</u> factor.

No one will ever target anything useless. Come to think of it, why should anyone undergo the rigor of decision making, why will companies pay heavy amount of money for panel of decision makers, there must be something motivating that sure! There is.

Now whether you have decided rightly or wrongly your decision must have what is known as ***identity***. I mean you and people around must see and feel your decision as to saying it is Mr. As decision. Take for instance the identity of president Musa Ya'adua in his administration was his amnesty to the Niger Delta region while the Decision of President Goodluck Ebele Jonathan to deploy more soldier to Abia state is the death of Osisika Nku and that is the identity.

The identity of your decision is a reflection of your ideology. You will also agree with this that no decision can ever work without appropriate negotiation and readiness to absorb any emanating negativity.

Moreover, decision making does not give room for negation at the middle of Execution least it must be in favor of the decision and above all, all decision is geared towards Achievement of the set target.

Before a decision can be made there must be concrete plan to Terminate or eliminate all obstacles capable of faulting the decision.

It is a known fact- that no one can venture into making a decision without Illuminating fully on that which is to be decided upon.

The only thing that is capable of making your decision firm is your ability to order for opportunities within Necessities. And decisions are made mostly on necessity and urgency or cogency.

Friends I present before you failure and achievement make your decision on which to choose don't forget. ... ***Die if you must provide is the will of your decision*** – only then you have made a decision.

EVALUATION

This happen to be another world found in the world of determination, in fact it is, a rare quality though common.

A Philosopher (Religious) once stated; unexamined life is not worth living – depending on how you view it, I think I totally concur with him; life here is in its totality.

Evaluation takes into consideration a lot of factors; it consults past, present and future with great emphasis on cause and effect.

In all, its consideration, its targets, in evaluating is for progression or redress. The evaluating minds that is after being into the world of determination does not take part in inductive reasoning, it will rather participate in deductive reasoning i.e. it considers all ways, all means, as ways and means until they prove not to be.

The evaluating minds are in life found in the profession of quality assurance and control. They work with a Target they consider all modules operandi – Executions and workability, with great Resistance to chance of Regret.

In evaluation, all Motivating factors are geared toward exposition of Identities that are not negotiable in the bead to achievement of the set target. During evaluation factors which terminated previous plans are looked into and given audience or terminating procedure provided. It involve a lot of consultation during which a lot is being illuminated and the evaluator without delay Order for the Illuminated opportunity with great emphasis on necessities. It must lay emphasis on necessity because you are still evaluating, and all opportunities must be in line to helping you arrive in 100% evaluation of what to target.

Friends if you are reading with rapt attention you will see that determination is like a chain and is set in life to be a ladder to whatever you wish to get in life. You can see that any of the quality treated gives way for the next attribute needed from you. I have never seen anybody who ascend a ladder and still stand on that climbed rail, you can only see it when you work back and the height will tell you, you will soon pass the next one.

...we are going to mount T.

Come on!

Come on!!

Follow me!!

TARGET

Wanderer; would be the football player without a goal post. Many will speak about target with various adjective, like, goal, dream, aim, objective whatsoever but what I am talking about or about to speak on is TARGET nothing more.

The target that is trapped in determination, I define thus: ***...It is an Identified, Executable & Achievable opportunities Motivated and illuminated amidst Necessities with strong will to Terminating obstacles resisting its actualization.***

Yes that is how I see it and it's exactly like that, everything you! yes you do in life you do it with a target, you go to toilet for a target, you even sleep for a target – invariably all that abide below the stars of the sky set Target.

The rich and the poor, young and old, Men and women, but the big and mostly a time unanswered question due to self deceit remains; is your target achievable? What is the mode of execution? It is only the foolish adventurer who will know that his or her target is scientifically, religiously and practically unrealistic and will still go ahead to set target.

The religious will say with God all things are possible, without thorough evaluation of the quote? "Do not put thy God the Lord to test" and you will set out to fly down from Mount Everest – your mentor could not do It.; reason best known to him. So, why not reason?.

You will set a target of converting the entire Nigeria into a fish pond – for the continent of Africa to grant you monopoly over the import and export of fish of all kind in and outside the globe. Forgetting that your mentor refuse turning stones into loaf of bread at the said time for a particular reason – in fact all his reason went through the ladder of his determination to redeem you.

I have concluded that people that set this kind of target are against the specific power and grace of Jesus Christ.

My advice to these set is ...*Dream if you must, but within the ambit of life target buried in determination.*

....*the greatest destroyer of purpose is setting a regrettable, non achievable, unmotivated, unidentified and un-illuminated, yet not negotiable opportunities within the midst of necessities – the end there of is termination.*

This is what I mean; a president of a certain country while on seat had a target for her nation which he tagged vision 2020 which is a fantastic thing.

But there is a lot of impediment limiting its actualization but because of sycophancy, selfish interest his advisers refuse to let him know of this limitations. Unfortunately, he met his death before his tenure elapsed. You may know the rest of the story I am not ready to talk politics here but what I want to bring out is that he died with his vision – because his vice who succeeded him never talked about it.

Even in his return for a full tenure of (4) four years, almost little or nothing is said about it. I presume some factors are responsible, maybe he cannot identify his motivating factor, or it is not well illuminated, may be the modus operandi is not there, it could be that there are more pressing necessities than that e.g. security, or facilities on ground is making the target unachievable, invariably it may be undergoing negotiation for termination and so it has become a regretful target.

...it is a dogmaCome all along!!
For we can never be there until we are there!!!

◆ ◆ ◆

EXECUTION

...your executing attitude is a reflection of your attainable altitude in life – it is a physical and experimental examination and identification of self will, strength, zeal and vigorous might within the vicissitudes of determination is not as if people do not dream and aspire for greatness – the point is that this remains the only lacking element in their dreams.

It is only when you understand fully what you want, that you can be able to have a comprehensive plan on how to get it and only then will your motivation keep increasing because you know what you are gunning for.

One of the continual questions put forth by intending helpers on our way to achieving life target or plan, is always - how do you intend to achieve this and your inability to convince such helper makes him see his help to you as being fruitless because you yourself lacks real commitment.

In one of my trips to Abuja, I met a very young school leaver who just wrote the University tertiary matriculation examination(UTME) – it reminded me of my days of struggle for admission, so I was moved to ask her young lady which course did you put in for? Food science she said, food science?....and technology!

Thrilled with her enthusiasm for a course that many underestimate, reject and neglect, that happened to be my course of study, I asked again; do you know what that course is all about? Yes off course she replied, are they not dietician, cooks, chiefs and nutritionist.

I looked at her again and smiled not knowing what to say because that is general opinion of what FST is all about, all I could tell her was this "my dear if really you are interested in studying food science and technology, go reschedule your plan because it is beyond cookery, dietary, and nutrition - in fact go back to mind your elementary physics, math's and chemistry as you will be involving in it at advanced level".

There and then she became frightened. What I am trying to say, her mode of executing FST as a profession is through cookery, dietary and the rest, by the time the course wires her with calculations she will have no choice than to accept a maximum of seven (7) years in what ordinarily with fore knowledge of what you want should be 4-5 years.

People fail to execute because of several factors but most exigent of them all are; in ability to resist limiting obstacles with quick resolution to take to regret on why they undertook the action in the 1ˢᵗ place.

This is a sign of non-enduring motivational factors as a result of not being able to identify that which is motivating you. It could also be lack of navigation power. When there is no alternative plan to getting to your destination, then you cannot negotiate other means and so takes to negativity of navigating between withdrawals and quitting.

Once you give in to negotiation with your Target, forget all plans because they become's lengthy and unnecessary. And this will invariably land you into terminating your link for achievement, as a result of inadequate illumination into the future-foresight within available opportunities you would have voluntarily ordered for, what a shame! In other to execute without regret your modus operandi must be vast.

I want to announce to you that every single problem has million and zillions of solution but you can't realize this until you see everything around you as a means. To execute without being executed involve having 26 means of execution i.e. making available plans A B to Z of possibilities and impossibilities and then, following up those you think are impossible because they are not, they are only trying to be tough and needed just two letter words to be decoded by you – *I.M* either as *"I* must", it must" "is master minding – *POSIBILITIES*.

The only thing you need in all you think that is impossible within the "I" and the *"M"* is manipulating M –man maneuver and manipulating all impossibilities – so they say needs you to maneuvering.

Are you executing! Do you want to execute!! Have you executed!!! Whichever stage you are currently, I urge you to stop and reconsider your plans – your modus operandi.

I assure you there must be a modicum for obeying this instruction – it is a dogma of determination you must execute like the determined.

Don't forget;
...the synergy of a man's exertion lies in his execution and what he executed.

◆ ◆ ◆

RESISTANCE

Resistivity is an important quality demanded by the world of determination. I do not care how you understand it but resistance is resistance. Listen, ***it is the resistivity of the rock over rain and all form of fluid that makes it impervious to liquid but a host to all valuable fluids.***

Determination demands that you posses great aversion for regret which appear like a crescent within your avenue. That thing you are having in mind, who tells you it comes so easy? Who says! Look between every two mountain there exist slopes.

Beside friends you can never get to the hill top until you create a path be it smooth or rough ones. Millions of dreamers, visionaries, fall of the track as a result of their inability to resist obstacles while in execution process many are often knocked down by the last sturdy in destiny.

Life is like a tunnel, fueled by determination constructed with crevices, your inability to identify and motivationally negotiate and navigate these crevices both illuminated, non-illuminated ones, and leaves you with chunks and lumps of regret capable of terminating the achievement of life opportunities.

The greatest weapon of resistance is necessity. The rock is quiet aware that it needn't much rain during the rainy season so it allows it go down the valley and get stored within the stream where it calls for it during dry season – if only we can learn from nature you and I, know too well that there is no life on Valueless Entities; so why not search for the value before seeking for LOVE – Living on Vague Ecstasy - is the surest way to doom.

What the hell is this guy saying?

Oh sorry!!!

do not be offended, I am not against LOVE, I am only saying, like the rock : avoid unnecessary pleasure because they are irresistible - if you are not conscious of it, and most sturdy of life comes in such clothing, if you don't watch it they will simply land you into bunch and baskets of regrets.

Resistance in the world of determination *is simply refusal to anything, all things, opinions, suggestions, anything of any kind which is not contributory to the will and wish of your decisions.*
Don't forget

...The most unfortunate cry of the unfortunate remains had I know. And the greatest weapon of resistance is necessity.

My word to you is this, why didn't you know, why had you not known, you had better known oh! In fact you have known that the cry of had I known is a regret to your in ability to resist while executing.

If you do not know, know it that the determined never cries had I known - because it is demoralizing, rather they will say; now that I know better? What next? – once you can cry this way opportunities will know, that you were successful in your failings and will present itself for retrial – recall that most letter in determination repeated itself for you to know that you can always have opportunity to Re-try.

Don't forget

...Coats and shells are protective walls to its possessor in your world of determination what is your shell of resistivity?

It is with great honor and in reverence to almighty and revelation of the Holy Spirit via the Holy Scripture that I unveil the protecting shell of some people. Hope you will identify yours. I have the double honor to welcome you to the undoubting quality called....***motivation***.

◆ ◆ ◆

MOTIVATION

The scripture says; my people suffer because of lack of wisdom and knowledge. I am pleased to announce to you that after this revelation; the heaven let loose and there fell from above the world of information technology, so ignorant no longer serves as a defense. Today my people no longer suffer and perish due to lack of knowledge but motivation.

It is with great displeasure that I inform you that your Aspirations perish because of lack of motivation. Beloved no doubt your Aspirations will compulsorily go into Expiration without inspiration, think about it.

Listen, your inability to identify your motivating factor will land you into deviation from your set target with little or no negotiation on possible escape route for better opportunities. Motivation remains the only product that has no expiration. I call it the fuel in the bus of achievements.

To be determined is to tactfully identify your motivating factors, power it tenaciously, service and maintain it without compromise.

Every other quality, factors can fail you, but your motivating factor can never fail you. It is the twin brother of your target, the engine in the bus of determination and the mechanic in the road of Execution. It is the only bulldozer in the field of determination, the pioneer of achievement and the illuminator of opportunities in the land of Necessities.

All creatures by nature are highly motivated, if not for any other thing; it will be because of achievement. It is the chief and the only cause of insatiability of man. It lures the achieved into pursuance of greater achievements and spurs the unachieved into aspiring for achievements. The urge for motivation is greater in people who have seen affluence but could not touch it. In fact most at times, the poor in the society are more highly motivated than the rich, find out. Many are of the opinion that the only motivation their target needs is finance, but I am very sorry to disagree with you as somebody who has been motivated before because money has about 10 – 20% role to play when it comes to motivation – it is a dogma of determination, i.e. how it is belief it or leave it. If you give higher % to money as your motivating factor you will achieve nothing in life.

I have seen children from well to do homes who with all their affluence return to the grass at the demise of their parents. Why? Because while in affluence there were no studs to motivate them not to talk about determination, any little thing, they will be the 1st to present a cheque- who said! Majority of them even take their inspiration from drugs and once, the billions needed for drugs are gone that marks their end.

Don't forget
…Never! You allow your Aspiration to go into Expiration as a result of lack of inspiration – Motivation. Until you are inspired you can't aspire and soon you will expire- think about it.

◆ ◆ ◆

IDENTIFICATION

You will agree with me that the 1st thing parents do to their newly born child is identification – reason being that you can never be identified until you identify- it is a dogma of determination. I.e. you are a core determinant of your identity. In the world of determination, until you are determined you can never achieve that with which you can be identified.

Identy & Time

Identity can change with time but after a very long time of expected change and it does not come, it remains permanent.

Take for instance the moment a fetus identifies with a woman, she in turn calls it "my baby". The moment it identifies itself as male or female it is called boy or girl which is the 1st world general identification- the parent then gives the child personal identification upon which he or she is to build a world of its own with the name.

It is said that people's name have great impact in their life and achievement. I do not know how much you believe in this, but I believe greatly in it. And this is why many parents take time to give their child a name especially mothers.

Rarely, do people change their name; if they do, it is in reference to the above or in view to changing their identity. In a nut shell, every determination must have an identity. In a simplified term your target must have an identity different from all other identities if you must be announced and conferred the honorary title of the DETERMINED.

Until your identity is known your target is negotiable and at the same time not illuminated so can never meet with opportunities.

In fact it is emphatically necessary that, before you commence your execution plans you make room for identification on your way to the land of determination. Always let your stand known in all facet of life.

Identification happens to be the 1st assignment God gave to humanity. Adam tour the whole garden of Eden without identifying anything that looks like him and he was said to be unhappy until

God hear his heart beat and took sympathy in his mood and took from him something to make something for him.

And Adam without delay identified it and called it woman bone of my bone, flesh of my flesh. The truth is that there is something lying dormant in you, which can only be awakened via your search for it – listen! the greatest gift of life to humanity is reasoning.

Your ideas remain the only Asset that can make or mar you. In Adam's ideology he never gave thought of any other thing below his standard, he knew he was specially made in likeness and image of somebody and that nothing in the garden is as unique as he is, so he passed the 1st test of not downgrading the Almighty to a common animal or plant – have you identified yourself?

The 1st identification demanded by determination is self identification. Once you know yourself and know the Asset in you then you can think of how best to utilize or lavish it.

It is only when you identify your attributes, qualities and potentials that you can set Achievable targets. Is it not a disdain for a cripple without legs to set a target of riding a bicycle or motorcycle.

Another identification demanded by determination is that of needs and wants; the mistake people make is trying to attend to their wants and paying little or no attention to their needs.
Look, provide your needs and it will lead you to a place where your wants presented themselves.

This is what I mean you have 36000 naira; you need a phone for communication as a student fine must it be blackberry or Nokia of E-series.

Yes I need it for browsing and research, who said? You need it for social gratification - when you can get a good phone of 10,000 and invest the remaining 26,000 that is exactly what I mean by identification of needs and wants.

One business man who was doing well woke one day and went for a loan in the Bank, because he was doing well bank gave it to him, he thought he has arrived and wanted to meet his wants instead of his need to boasting and expanding his shop; so he went and bought a Land cruiser Jeep – it wasn't long bad market set in, he started using little returns from his goods to pay bank interest today the jeep is nowhere within his reach and his shop is almost empty; leaving your needs for your wants.

General Identification is the most demanded of all identity. If you cannot be identified with a target forget it. Once you identify your target you must illuminate it clearly for the public to understand it because;

the opportunity you are looking for is in the public and if you and your identity is not known to the public, in times of necessity nobody will remember you.
…..my identity is my self esteem buried in my name, my fights is to protect it while all my struggles is to sell it to the universe from my world.

◆ ◆ ◆

NO NEGOTIATION

In the city of determination negativity is prohibited no negotiation, because it had earlier been done before you decided, so if there must be any form of negotiation it must be in line with the will of your decision.

It simply means if you must be given the crown of determination never you call for negotiation press on until you are called for negotiation it is only then that you can meet your target.

Once you begin to negotiate on your achievement plans, two things are involved either you forfeit your achievement, or is slashed for you – this is more reason you should not call for it but be called. For you to be determined means that your target is non-negotiable.

To successfully tour through the street of determination, you must understand all principles of negotiation and navigation, like earlier stated, there are a lot of studs on every road that leads to your target and your ability to negotiate or even terminate them to the will of your decision makes you an achiever.

If you must have indent knowledge of the kind of negotiation demanded of you consult, government offices for contracts, or private contractors and most essentially climbers they will give you a life testimony.

Friends, if you have decided to achieve, succeed or meet your target, then you must avoid any form of negativity because it is the initiator of Negotiation. The only killer of motivation!-Terminator of achievers within the gates of achievement.

It never comes until you are about a meter away from your target and mostly at the last seconds of the last minute. It greatest enemy is motivation and the only mode of its destruction is further re-illumination or flash back in the motivating factor and a brief citation of already passed and crossed qualities in the city of determination.

Go back to our numeracy of determination, you will find out that is in the 7th position and 7 is known as a perfection number.

Again immediately after it comes the number one cause of our life struggle the indisputable and indispensable **ACHIEVEMENT** – it simply means that at that time the only thing needed of you is a show of perfection which will lunch you into your target. Just at this time say to yourself, all I need now is to put finishing touches – is now your right T. B. A.

Don't forget
...*negotiate if you must but it must be in favor of your target and in line with your decision.*

The hour has come, ladies and gentlemen, learned and unlearned, literates and illiterates, young and Old, I have the total honor to invite you to dine with the number one citizen of the world, the only cause of life struggle, join me as I welcome **MR.... *achievement*.**

◆ ◆ ◆

ACHIEVEMEMT

Would it be of any use trying to convince you of the universal quest for achievement? I will if that will make you to aspire to achieve.

Now know it, that even the insane man in the street wants to achieve; if this is not so why do you think he or she visit refuse dumps and gather all sort of things? Just try collecting any of those properties from him! Have you ever seen lactating Lunatics, they will rather die than to see you take away their baby with force- think about it.

Achievement is a universal need that only few can afford to pay the price but all wants it.

If you think that achievement is only for the dotty, well am serious to disappoint you as it not so, is also for the weak, it only requires a little synergy from your current practice.

Achievement is hyper friendly but the path that leads to it is wavy "waggy" and at the same time wades- achievement path is w.w.w.com i.e. wadi wavy waggy, but you will agree with me that there is no information that cannot be accessed within the www search engine. Importantly, achievement is highly accessible if only you can see the valley in which achievement is hidden, and then you can order for enough fuel (motivation) which will assist you in illuminating all obstacles necessary for termination before you can access achievement in the valley.

Just take a review of all the qualities demanded of you by determination, and that will tell you the depth for which achievement was buried in determination. Unless you are ready to dig deep, you can never exhume achievement.

Your preparedness is tested right from D – N and once you prove capable, then you have nothing to hold you back from falling into the valley of achievement where you will be shielded and protected by what? Don't worry you will soon understand.

NUMERACY OF ACHIEVEMENT

It is quite obvious that number happens to be the surest asset to which we can force determination to vomit that which it swallowed.

Recall that in numeracy of determination Achievement was found in 9th position with unique number nine (9) and numerated as an odd number (1) –it continued in this order to ascend and descend after great point, a peak has been attained.

Watch out A=1, C=3, H=8, I=9, E=5, V=22, E=5, M=13, E=5, N=14, T=19 in a sequential manner.

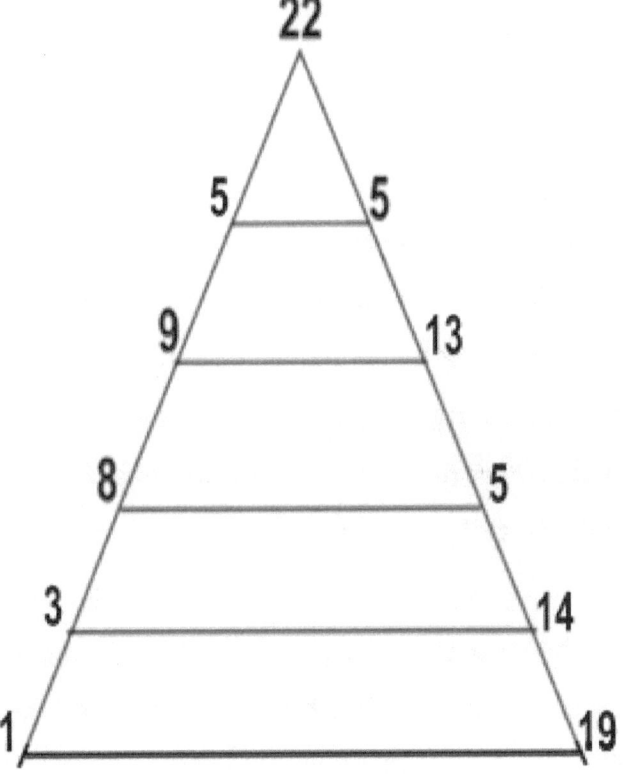

It poses the unique quality of yet an old number in its numeracy.

If you count the letters it is 11 and the middle number is the highest number.

Achievement is a Gradual process – the sequential numeracy in achievement is a clear indication that it is a gradual process and that you can never count 3 without counting one (1) the omission of 2,4,6, & 7 means that you are permitted to jump a step or two but you must begin with one.

It also implies that in your way to achieving your target there must be countless fall – it not a taboo but it is an abomination to fall without picking up something while standing or something that will enable you to stand.

◆ ◆ ◆

EVENNESS IN SUCCESS

The peak of the above pyramid is a clear indication that everybody has equal opportunity to excel. It at the same time sounds a warning to you that, that point you are standing is not personal. That anybody can take up the same position anytime any day i.e. it is a dual position for you and one other person. The achieved will tell you better and this is why the rich want to get richer, and will never allow you come up or get to their secret of being there because they are aware that life offers even achievement opportunity and this is why the majority of them are sincerely with their heat stand-offish – aloof towards like minds and potential achievers.

STABILITY IN ACHIEVEMENTS

The stability in achievement is highly dependent on mode of attainment/acquisition and how you handle your achievement.

The sharp drop in value from 22 to 5 simply means that; that you have achieved does not mean you cannot fall. It also infers that even the achieved can still fall without stud faster than you, you can imagine, and this is why it did not follow sequential order. But any achievement that is a product of determination hardly falls.

ASSURANCE OF ACHIEVEMEMT

The great assurance given by achievement through determination is that you will hardly fall, if you must fall it can never be below your starting point-it is a double assurance. It is seen in the repetition of the figure 5 and not starting with 21 to descend.

The sharp rise and fall indicates that the taste of achievement will never allow you to remain at your fallen point, so you are bound to rise again with speed and with speed will you fall again, until you review your determination factors, then you will rise again gradually without limitation.

What is this guy trying to feel like? Does he think it is so easy; why does he speak with so much confident? My dear questions no more, see it yourself in a graph – it is a dogma of determination.

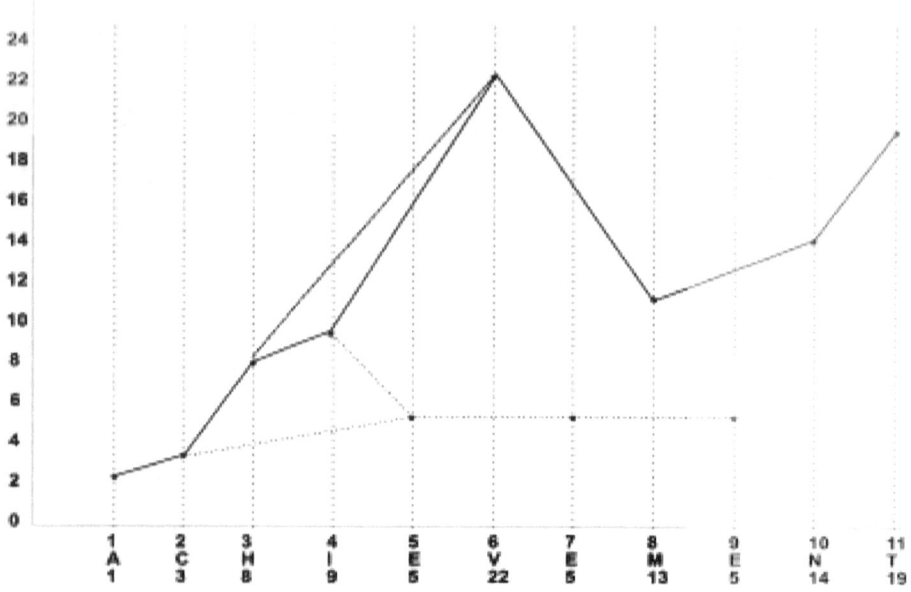

SCHEMATIC OF ACHIEVEMENT

Does this convey any meaning to you; can you now understand all I have said before that graph? If you don't sorry! I have been mandated to say more just keep following the ink.

I do not want to know how you interpret the graph but I wish to point out few important features of that graph; the thick path and the thin path, like I said paths, choose which to follow. Again, along the paths are stages of achievement – wait a minute, they are not just path they are achievement pathway.

THE ACHIEVEMENT PATHWAY

I am comprehensively convinced that majority will like to follow the smoothest and short–dotted path. Yes people that want to jump and pass; short cut mongers. I will advise you to follow the thick path – because I have never seen a vehicle that speeds while ascending a hill no matter how the driver fires or accelerates. If that happens, the rate of ascending will definitely equal that of descending.

Beside look at where you are going to, the peak is too sharp for you to rest on if you take to it surely before you get to the top you must rest and in achievement city there is no room for rest – people will pull you down! If not people, because you are resting gravity will finish you and your next available option will be nothing else but deceleration.

Beloved if you must aim for the peak of achievement, then toe the path of gradual process, it will be of immense help to your retaining the top.

STAGES OF ACHIEVEMENT

No doubt achievement has stages and you are permitted to make the choice of your desire stage. Majority will prefer to attain the guarantee stage-xxx, some will attempt following the gradual path many will succeed while many will fall to the assurance stage and that fear of falling below their starting point will never allow them to rise again.

No matter your chosen stage, there must be one or two falls; if your achievement was through determination then you can never fall below your starting point.

Don't forget
…you can never achieve all that you want to achieve but must achieve all that you have determined to achieve.

It's a dogma of determination, join me as we introduce yet another virtue demanded by determination, the twin brother of target, defender of achievements and promoter of the determined, in person of Mr. Terminatio.

❖ ❖ ❖

TERMINATION

Please the termination demanded by determination here is not abortion. Termination in its simplicity means to end something in reality; all life obstacle aims at either ending you or ending that which you are targeting. It is therefore paramount that you acquire skill that will aid their termination – End those obstacles of any kind before they end you.

Obstacles! obstacles!!!

I know you will be placing your mind only on physical sturdy, you! Yourself- is a great obstacle.

You can be giving yourself, your targets, an unbeatable stud, without knowing.

How do you want to achieve your target when you spend all your life earning in the beer parlor and on a bed with different kinds of woman, what do you think you can achieve in that your wank – life?

where you useless all the energy that could be invested into meaningful thoughts or you lesbian and homosexual to mention but a few.

Look!! the first determination in your life will be ending those ill values and vices before they end you.

❖ ❖ ❖

It's true that if we know the consequences of what we do a times, we will never do it but light has come into the world to illuminate those things that eluded people in the past.

The true meaning of determination can never be found until you are able to terminate obstacles - challenges -your ability to put to an end pressing issues within a necessity, is a measure of your determination.

They are ready to terminate you if you do not have de-termination in other words; **DE-TERMINATION IS AN ANTIGEN FOR TERMINATION.**

Friends, I charge you today to detonate, de-terminate those things masking you from or masking your opportunities, terminate them and order those masked opportunities because it has been fully illuminated.

Even the achieved make use of the principles of termination and that is why it is demanded by determination.

Have you wondered why owners of industries fire their staff or mangers? It's no reason, other than terminating you, who is not meeting the set target before you terminate them and their business.

That your boss in the company can never grant your study leave because he is only but HND holder and when you return with your masters' degree his position will be at risk. That MR. (PhD) will pull him down because his project work is fantastic so will encourage and favor his publication for professorship

so giving you a good grade will put the work into open attraction within the senate, the external supervisor and the science world at large; End those things before they end you - To de-TERMINATE is to offend.

In the world of determination, if you must be a terminator you must learn how to be an offender not a defender. Believe me that most defenders get tired and will often loose out.

The administration of Nigeria and some other nations today are majorly, occupied and manned by those who their religion instructs to be offenders. For instance the scripture says if any one slaps you in one check give him the other for him to tap or smash, I mean! – forgetting the fact that the Kingdom of God suffers violent and man of violent takes it by force.

When the offender i.e. those who their religion tell to kill their killer before they kill them understand the former injunction, they often take to the offending side before the defenders wake to the philosophy of violence it is already too late because the offender had taken cover, defender will always loose because the offender knowing that you will defend plans ahead of you and even beyond your defense while you are yet to understand his attacks because you can't defend without understanding.

Hey! Men watch it!!

I am not preaching violence here, neither am I saying you should go down the street fighting all in the name to offend so as to provide that, been demanded of you by determination No! No!! NO!!!

All am trying to say is deal with those obstacles, those challenges before they start dealing with you why because your defense may be less felt.

Meanwhile do not ever offend when you know you can never gain victory. **Offending is best when if you don't offend, you will be offended -** avoid any chance that can land you into defending. *Don't forget*

....determination demands that you must be an offender rather than a defender if you must de-Terminate successfully
– it is a dogma of determination learn it.

◆ ◆ ◆

Hello!
Is someone still catching up?

I am glad to know you are still there.

It's a long journey isn't it?

Yes off course its only after going through it that you can look at anybody with eyes of determination just like I do when i see people sing;

...I have decided to follow Jesus ....I have decided...and I will reply it is easier said, than to doo....
why not determines... to follow Je...sus!

Who is deceiving who? That you just took the D. who "ETERMINE"?

-it is dogmas of determination live it.

ILLUMINATION

Imagine what the entire body will be like without the eye, I mean be in the shoes of the blind for once. Although the blind never feel the terror of the night but the absence of light increase their pain.

The dictionary defines illumination as; light or place that light comes from, and also as an understanding or explanation of something. And the Christian scripture says you are light of the world and salt of the earth. It simply means that you are a source of light, an embodiment of understanding, you are an explanation to one of God's creatures:

Necessities present you with darkness and as a light you are to light up all darkened areas in search of opportunities.

Being the light of the world does not mean that the moon, the stars and the sun have been relieved of its duties. Neither does it mean that you are now a candle that people should light up before they can sea.

It simply implies that there are luminous elements in you capable of illuminating the world i.e. giving explanation to certain earth phenomenon and creature.

It does not mean that you should set naked fire or go into nuclear bombing because you can illuminate the world. It's a call for service to the universe, to use that which He deposited in you for the positive advancement of the world we leave in. And the world will forever wait for your invention patiently.

I want to announce to you that you have one or two object to explain on this earth. One or more people must be able to understand you and get illuminated via your luminosity.

THE GREATEST PRISON OF THE WORLD

The greatest prison of the world is found in humanity. I am aware that many people often neglect those with visual disability thinking that, they are incapable of illuminating the earth. Now let me inform you that the worst kind of blindness is "Mind blindness" and this is the world's greatest prison.

The call of determination is to get your mind globally illuminated. It has never been heard of any mind that has not the luminosity of nature, the big question is has darkness taken over it. Bear it in mind, that your luminosity is not felt or seen in you but in the objects and substances under your illumination- i.e. those things you can be said to have done at time of necessity those things that when people illuminate in their world, they will remember the person behind it which is you!

Your inability to light up the blind mind of any forms is clear indication of your non-luminosity, which means you need to be illuminated – you are an opportunity.

I don't think I have ever seen black salt! All salt I have ever seen come in almost white color and white is luminous in nature – imperatively you can never be salt of the earth if you cannot illuminate the earth, opportunities. Come to think of it!

How do you intend to give taste to the earth as a salt, when you cannot be seen as a dark and blind mind or anything can be seen which is traceable to your identity? Come on! You're too watery go regain your salinity via determination, which will take you under the sun to charge you and dry up some of the excess water in you that made you tasteless.

Light gives confident, hope and a kind of fulfillment, so as light as somebody under the call of determination you must be luminous and not just stop there, go ahead to illuminate into the life and darkest mind of people so as to restore their confident, lost hope and low self esteem.

Finally, bear it in mind that nobody in this world who is in its right frame of mind-follow darkness everybody is in search of light because it is good and attractive. So until you illuminate that your targets that which you want to achieve, it remains unattractive and therefore not achievable.

You are quite aware that the world is ruled by these two agents; that of Darkness and that of light, but am glad and at the same time sad to inform you that even the agents of darkness make use of the light.

So if you have refused to illuminate those beautiful potentials in you, it will turn dark and once that happens, I assure you agents of darkness will never miss making adequate use of you. If you doubt this, consult atheist, gentlemen of the high ways, and off cause the occult kingdom.

I guess equally that this is the cause of using God given potentials in professional field against humanity and nature-with contextual scientific ideas, legal abortion, tube fertilization and the rest of them making no big deal to perpetrators.

Don't Forget
...the greatest disease is not that which kills the body but that which kills the mind – Non luminosity of the mind and resistance to illumination is an incurable disease.

It is a dogma stick to it – "determination remains the only known cure to the disease of the mind" think about it.

ORDERING FOR OPPORTUNITES

Every illuminated mind likes its eyes opened and focused to necessities, and within it, it see opportunities with no delay, no negotiation and orders for them immediately as a man of determination he is.

It is off the non-illuminated to wait for opportunities, for the illuminating minds, opportunities wait for them all they do is to order for it. It only takes a man of determination to order for opportunities, they are never ordered with force or any other thing other than self-assertiveness in your determinations.

Those who "order for opportunities" see failing as an opportunity to succeed better than they have just done. They will rather say am not there implies that, more is demanded from me.

Rather than say I have supplied what is needed to put in, my best because I was already there, instead of "I tried my best what else does it want from me? I can't kill myself for it – if you cannot kill your mug self for it, then try something else, something you are determined to achieve because not being ready to kill yourself for it implies that you can't die for your decision

Show me a man of determination, I will present to you a man of great achievement with vast opportunities that he never miss to achieve from.

Dear reader, just look at the path we have journeyed before arriving to the world of opportunity. Does it communicate anything to you?

To me, I think determination presents you with a lot of challenges to bring out the best in you in handling opportunities before it presents itself. It means that, anyone who posses all the qualities presented before now, can never miss or miss handles opportunities.

Opportunity is like a trust and before someone gives out his or her trust he makes thorough assessment of your trust worthiness. In-fact, I now stand very firm without any atom of doubt in me to tell you that determination is the only secret to achieving anything you sole determined to achieve.

Determination is only tested in hard-difficult works or tasks. Do not take any of the earlier treated qualities for granted. As they presented themself-sequentially within the street of determination, that is how they will appear in every opportunity and if the opportunity availed to you is not earned via determination you will surely miss it- this is why the best inventors of this world, record breakers are never known to come from the over well to do families because wealth blind fold their thinking aid get their mind and brain blocked with pleasure of achievement presented by achievement itself to those who stumbled into it, the money bags, and money miss roads.
Don't forget
…Joseph was presented with such pleasures by achievement itself.
His refusal landed him to the street of determination where he

met with opportunities amidst necessities and he had a second encounter with achievement again, then he gained mastery over it.

Know it today that that which you call achievement may really be a litmus test for your destined achievement.
Don't forget.

Illuminate your mind within necessities; you shall see opportunities calling for you, order for them with personal weapon of assertiveness.

NECESSITIES

Yes, it is necessity that is said to bring invention but there can't be any invention without determination because necessities are buried and swallowed up in determination.

In the world of determination, there is nothing or a word like unnecessary - the fact that it as unnecessary makes it a necessity calling for determination. You are busy looking for the necessary things, getting behind the one you feel is unnecessary forgetting that it is "un"-one in French code that is masking your necessities.

All you need is the determination; once you are illuminated within the street of determination, people and necessities will trace you when the need of you arises amidst opportunities.

I am quite sure that many do not understand what it means to have a necessity. It is true as in a de-facto that everything that is unavoidable is a necessity but to all, no matter what happens around you never call it a necessity until there is a need for your presence.

Men and women of determination never present themselves to necessities that want their presence but those that need their presences, not for any other reason other than the fact that there are a lot of opportunities they can have ordered for. You will agree with me that everybody want to be with the achieved, but everybody does not necessarily need to be with the achieved-in doing so they miss their opportunity of achieving. In the city of determination, there is always a long term provision for necessity.

It is only the prepared who make invention within necessities, those who await necessities with preparedness i.e. knowing fully well that there must be necessities they often utilize opportunities provided by it, better than those who are charged by necessities – why do governments make provisions for reserve, foreign and local, internal and external.

The crabs says that it presents its nostril before its eyes, so as to perceive necessity call for him to run before he sees the war - because its journey is like that of a big man, is not swiftly.

The tortoise then ask him but we engage in the same kind of walk - in reply the crab said yes, but we are not of the same shell, when people step on your shell you easily takes in your head but for me; I suffocate in the mud shedding tears that gives no blood, no matter how hard I claw and clip on their feet.

Friends why not like the crab, learn to see necessities before it sees you, that "A" survived within necessities without a prior plans does not mean you will also be fortunate like "A" but you become more fortunate if you prepare and wait for opportunities that comes with necessities.

Don't forget

....the easiest way to win a battle is to take a cover in preparedness before the war front.

It's a dogma of determination take it or you consult the soldier in war trench.

It is pleasant to know that you have endured to the end it is a clear indication of your desire to be determined.

I hope you have learnt, one or two things, or seen enough reason to apply the principles of determination in that which you are about to conceive.

Know it that it is only difficulties that can prove your determination and that each virtue in here has been proven.

With the power rested on me as the carrier vessel of this microscopic element, I have been mandated to present and deliver to your conscience the only know. Test for determinations – the small but mighty **Mr. DIFFICULTIES** – the most popular guy in the world of execution the public relation officer of determination.

DETERMINATION IS TESTED IN DIFICULTIES

Difficulties are defined as things or situation with a lot of problems. They are often not easy to deal with and often require a lot of efforts and skills.

In other words you can never be said to have determination without acquisition and display of your experiences - It is the level of skill and effort put in during difficult times that make the world to see your determination.

Do you now see why the children of the aristocratic status hardly gain determination? All those who have been or are currently in the field of determination have one or two experience to share about tough and challenging situations, if I should share all I have experienced, that often tend to proof tougher than my skill, you can never decide to be determined.

Not only that I have seen though situations, in fact other peoples difficult experiences coupled with my little one, have made me to visualize determination as a trench – if I show you the picture of people determination to overcoming challenging situations, then you will understand why it remains the only key to unlocking uneasy situations.

To be honest with you, I will not hide anything or fact from you just like most foreign authors will present you with only those things that will motivate your psych,

I will present the facts for you to take your decision and make it firm. Be patient while I introduce you to the path of determination. It is only then you will appreciate the fact that difficulties are the true test for determination.

THE PATH OF DETERMINATION

It is a path engulfed with difficulties. A www path, it seem not easy so the end thereof is not condemnation but recommendation. It is a wonky-wavy-wadi path. We shall make reference to numeracy of determination against the position of the letters in it.

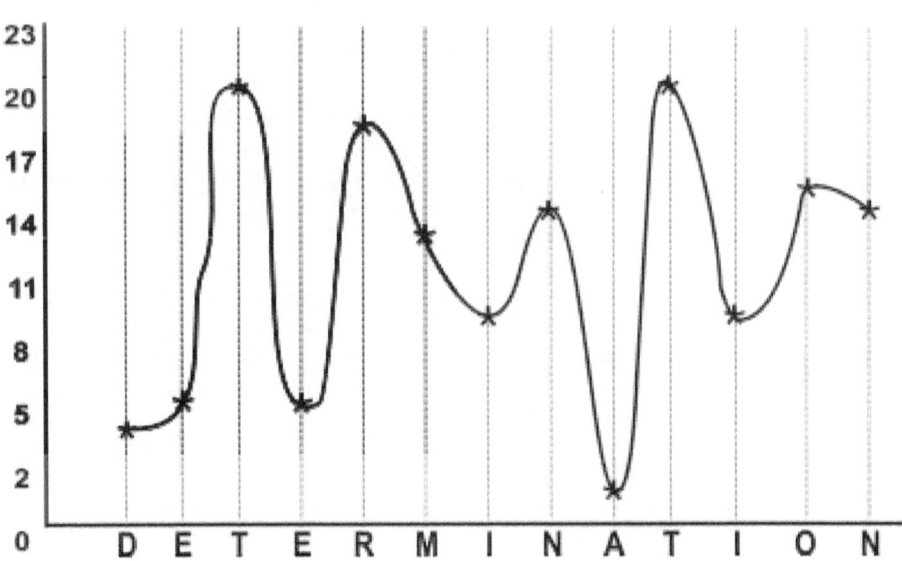

Yes, this is exactly the way of determination, no matter how you view it, no matter how you approach it; it is not, because it never appeared easy. If you like view it as a path on a platform i.e. horizontally, it is yet very rigorous and even appeared more difficult because you can't see where you're going to until you approach a bend. The other way round, if your view it as a mountainous path, it will demand a lot of courage from you to ascend it. There is no way you move the path of determination that it appears easy; yet I will like you to view it as a mountainous path, because it appears closer and faster too-but demanding.

The path posses a lot of features if you look at the starting point, point of decision making, it's a beat smooth making it available for all. It is a point where nobody knows what is going on in your mind, in fact no one sees you until you achieve the point of visibility.

The point that you can say to yourself I have decided to achieve this target – simply put, it is a stage of invisibility you do not see and you are not seen, the mountainous target shields you.

From the invisible stage you can see that the only way out is through evaluation. Evaluation will lead you to making a decision of whether to set a target or to consider other decisive options.

◆ ◆ ◆

POINT OF VISIBILITY

On your path to determination you can never see, nor can you be seen until you reach to the peak where you have set a target from your evaluation.

It is at this point that you stand upright and see far ahead and all you will see will be below you, this is the point where you stand and site achievement in your set target.

If you can see, you will see another wall standing behind achievement and your mind will tell you once I achieve that that's all! That ends it all!! Well let me inform you that, that which is the wall ending all achievement is not as you thought; it's but a monitor, a terminator. It monitors and aims at all that has climbed the mountain of target. It watches you go through the hills and valleys before achievement, without harming you if only you have plan to overpower it.

The main responsibility of the mountain of termination is to watch over achievement. It monitors with great care those who want to approach achievement from N. Short cutters, fast guys, it hardly fights you because it believe that you both are far apart, that before you get to achievement you will surely be exhausted or even give up but with motivation you can always grab at termination and make great use of it.

Beloved if you do not know, *know it now that you remain invisible until you set a target. Also you can never be aimed at for termination until you are seen. Moreover, nobody is interested in terminating you but your targets.* Until you set a target, you can't see the possible terminators of life.

The protective mountain of termination seen as a wall is a clear indication that there is no short cut to achievement, if you toe the end path-that leads to termination; you may suddenly see achievement but must taste the arrows of termination.

◆ ◆ ◆

BEING IN THE DEPTH OF ACHIEVEMENT

Throughout the whole universe, I have toured through all that exist in life that is seen as valuable. I have never seen anyone that is said to come from the peak of hills or mountain.

The only thing peak of mountains does is drag-often gravity. Take a close look at the graph, you will see that target and achievement are inversely opposite, in fact achievement hidden itself in the depth sea of determination.

I have come to discovered that must valuable things are found in the depth. The presence of minor depths, before the ultimate depth that housed achievement is serving as a training to going deeper into the depth of achievement.

If you are told how deep the driving bit goes before it get crude oil, then you will understand how deep you need to dig, to dip your cup of achievement in the world of determination.

Don't forget
…the riches of the earth are found in the depth, so dig deep to overcome the fear of the depth.

◆ ◆ ◆

MY JOURNEY INTO THE DEPTH OF ACHIEVEMENT

Several times have I been to the street of determination and countless times have I been trapped in the depth of achievement. If I begin to ink it, your brain and mind will comprehend it not, will not contain it. But to give life to the practicability of what you read in this book I shall narrate my experience while journeying down the depth of achievement.

The only thing I want you to learn from what you are about to explore is this;
the road leading to success may at the beginning seem lonely but look well you will surely see the foot print of people who have treaded it, you will soon discover that the end thereof is crowded; you are only coming behind, encouragement will only come if you refuse to give up.

MY CANDIDACY IN THE PRESIDENCY

As a believer, people especially fellow believer see it as being canal that participation in political activities but I saw leadership as Christian neglected and abandoned ministry that have contributed to the consistent suffering of children of God. I know I have this enduring passion for service to humanity especially with great sense of justice equity and fairness.

With respect to personal integrity, prestige and self esteem, *I believe you can never be well or better if your society is in jeopardy – you can only be well by making the society well for others.*

In-fact knowledge backed with experience without impacting to the environment is a menace to the society. And at the same time *the greatest injustice to humanity is refusal to do that which you are capable of doing to effect the environment positively.*

Beside the treasure in us is meant for the world not for ourselves, we are only but the protective host. So after a talk (an exaltation) in one of my ministerial camping retreat in Ado-Odo Ogun State Nigeria, the guest speaker spoke with divine inspiration of the holy spirit and strong proves from the scripture on Gods ordination of Leadership ministry, there and then I decide that whenever duty calls, for my service in any leadership, position anywhere in the world, I must respond positively and effectively to it.

It was not long after this decision I gained admission into the one and the only Federal University of Technology in the whole of the South-South, South West, South East, sub Sahara within the jaws of the Limpopo, Federal University of technology Owerri.

Right from my point of registration into the students Union as a freshman, I saw a lot of abnormalities that I can single handedly normalize even as fresh intake.

I began to enquire, to investigate into the causative cause of lost of sagacious sagacity in the mind of political elites within the Union and the university management who have become kleptomaniac with the fortune and wealth's, with great neglect to fundamental right of my fellow Nigerian students who elected them into office for public defense of these right and privileges.

My findings presented me with a dying need for Acculturation within the Union leaders and the entire members who have no means of communication, to talk of accountability to the members of the Union by its officers.

I also discovered that Union members have lost hope and interest in the Union to the point that for the members it is; "my dear you have to learn to leave with what you can't change" and to the energetic visionary aspirants elected into the office of the union it is; "if you can't beat them! You join them".

Isn't this a looming danger for the Nation? If this happen in a breeding ground of future leaders, what is the future of the nation? What kinds of leader will emerge from this kind of society in two decades to come? I said to myself, NO! This can't be! Its call for ministration, a mission to restore the lost confidence in the union and make it leader regain it lost value for an assured general and not personal victory in Aluta struggle.

I took courage with my finding that all is given equal opportunity to do something about the ugly situation starting from 200 levels to 500 levels.

It is *TIME* for *REJUVENATION* of Aluta Spirit! vying for a post in student Union government ought to be a panacea to what politics looks like outside the university environment, but I can vividly tell you that it is harder than what happen in the Government of the federation especially office of the Union President, here is my experience.

Recall that I earlier told you that money contributes a minute percentage to that which you think that is your set back in achieving is money – sure! Because you have seen it as a setback, it will surely set you back. Throughout my consultation before I commence the race, a lot were listed for me as the requirement and to top in the list was finance.

I often give the full assurance that I have all the money it takes to run the office and win it. Meanwhile, I have just three thousand naira N3000 when I declared for the Office of Mr. President, I was not deterred or perturbed by it, because my confidence in determination to fulfill that which my mind tells me that I can, never failed me.

So I wore the garment of determination which served as my guide down the depth. And I want to tell you that I supplied all the qualities demanded from me by determination and at the end I was seen as determined. Here are my supplies to the demands.

DECIDING

I went through various series of decisions the 1st being should I or should I not run? Is true you are determined, but if you run will you will and why do think you will win? Yes this was all that presented itself that gave me the conviction that I can.

EVALUATING

I took a close look at those questions in order to decide correctly I gave genuine and sincere answers. I checked out what will make me unique and outstanding from all other candidates and singled out sincerity of purpose and determination to fight the cause down the depth – My aim was restoring the lost confidence to the electorates.

TARGETING

What I have decided to run is one thing, that I will win is another phase altogether. The post to run for was another point of decision which has great effect on my winning – Many saw me cable of manning different offices in the union, in-fact the only post that was not suggested for me to contest for was the sport directorate, that of social and those left for ladies.

This helped me in making decision about my target – that if the student can see potential in me fitting into all the offices, that I can then manage all the offices in one office. I did not neglect their suggestions, I put all of them into consideration, I still came to one point that I can never make the kind of impact I want to make in the union, in any other office other than that of the office of the President

Recall in our discussion on decision we said it's personal. It was a perfect decision, no one doubted my competence. They all saw the vitality in having my potentials invested in the union, then arose an obstacle, a 'but', having set the target of restoring confidence of the electorate to believe in the union, in the office of the presidency - "You are good to go but you are not an indigene!

The presidency was not the target, **Nigerian students were my interest, and the passion for defending their fundamental right, providing monumental and infrastructural needs was my drive.**
Executing

Yes! I have said I will! And the "you won't" has sprang up. Every aspirant was expected to canvas single handedly for vote until he or she gets people who believe in his or her cause.

Two things speak volume in gaining support, which are: money-for the sycophants,' competency for persons of like minds. Second was the possibility of success. The fact that I hadn't money was over looked by supporters, the emphasized on my competency and the possibility non indigene being allowed to serve as the union president even if I win.

It was the only visible obstacle seen by all. It posed great challenges before me. It served as propaganda against me, opponents capitalized on it and many saw me as a joker who is competent but have refused to believe or take reality cannot be accepted by the management.

I was among the first topmost candidates, yet my co aspirants never fought me they were busy fighting themselves while I was allowed to battle with the stigma of non indigene.

The truth is that this was not a formal disposition. Ask any FUTOites, he or she will tell you the rest of the story.

Resisting

it was one big task resisting this stigma meanwhile my course mates had earlier o warned that if I embark on the office of president I should expect their 50% support but if is that of P.R.O or any other, that I will have their 100% support that they would not like their effort to be vain-for me I better waste the effort than being a menace to the FUTO environment when I know I have something to offer.

I resisted their dissuasion went on with my decision, am glad to announce to you that I never regretted for a seconds. As I approach people, they kept on resisting me. Some will even tell me; why are you wasting your precious time?

Why not contest for another post or better still divert your competency into something more beneficial? Can't you see that even if the management can never allow that to happen? I persisted sooner than later my determination exposed my competency the more, and non indigenes were provoked, they began to fight my cause at my absence a lot of controversies rose in various points of gathering most especially on my appearance. So many were like why should it be like so? The stigma was a big challenge, I had go into research and discovered that a non indigene had once served as the union president, not even of the south east region (non Igbo) and his government appeared one of the best ever experienced since inception, his government did not permit manipulation from the management.

It gave the union the real Aluta spirit. This made the management to pick interest in who will serve as the union president. And this made indigenous aspirants to often use this reason to elude the mind of more competent non indigenous aspirant in the office of the president and the unenlightened.

I also discovered that a particular office has aided this evil stigma. I took advantage of my findings, went into classes to present my evidences- I tell you from that point I began to amass great number of supporters indigenes and non indigenes alike because the more I move the more my determination expose my hidden potentials.

◆ ◆ ◆

Action of Resistance

When my name went to number one and two, of the most preferred candidate, I feared I might be screened out by the stigmatizing office, I went to a higher office- the office of the pro chancellor to the university and was ready to ascend to that of the university chancellor which I already book appointment to that effect in Abuja should I not be answered in his office.

This was a great synergy for me as a lot of people were infused with fear because I came back with assurance that if I wins and am refused the office, the pro chancellor will intervene.

The talk on campus was that-he will not win! His strongest opponent is being supported by his HOD and even the dean of students' affairs wants him! And so! He (Mr. E.T.C) is been supported by the university pro chancellor, even the vice chancellor recommended him in the church.

… if you do not plan for the worst, you are bound to be in the worst and settle for the worst. If you forget all I have said in this page do not forget that a present messenger is more influential than the absent chairman or president.

And that the absent manager will believe his representative than any other. When the field marshal tells the general that all is well, it takes a lot from the captain to convince him that all is not well. *Don't forget*

…. It is better to have a secretary as friend than have the boss as a confidant.

Motivating

The race became too demanding, a lot was needed from me, the conviction that I must win had started coming. People now believe they must eat me before I start eating their wealth and fortune-the ancient unbelievers of acculturation those that can't trust themselves talk of trusting others.

I was not daunted, rather gained more motivation from my target; the hunger to restore confident in the mind of the electorates, the dying need for acculturating the minds that had been made to believe in wrong philosophy of what leadership in the union is- I neither offered bribe nor succumb to the frivolous financial demand of some group.

The people saw that I meant business, the next propaganda was he wants to achieve without vomiting! "It's those who vomit all that is in their pulse that eat to refill when they get to office" was my counter.

Look!

Once you have genuine motivator found in sincerity of purpose, I bet you money will not, can never be a deterrent to getting to your set targets.

◆ ◆ ◆

SELF MOTVATION

Without self conviction, there can never be motivation, once you're not motivated, you cannot motivate others and leaders are motivators! I needed to win general acceptability of all. So I came all the way from a different point. My conviction came from what I thought and knew can be brought to actuality. So I presented it to the students.

They needed no juggler convince them, as I motivated them to believing that the problem of the union can be met with or without focusing on the management. Within the possible period I saw some students praying for my success, as days goes by, their confidence in me grew yonder.

Remember we said...***knowledge backed with experience not impacted to the public is a menace to the society.*** Beloved, I want to inform you that even my fellow contestants saw some elements of sincerity of purpose in me. Just because of motivation, moral I earned massive support.

Three were screened out of the race, they all gave me their support and transferred their fans to me, even before then, during my presidential debate I left the entire students a flabbergasted as I made them understand I was going there to defend their neglected rights and privileges, to right the wrongs mated on them.

On the debate ground without any fear of intimidation, I countered the ISEC commissioners who wanted to monetize and turn the debate into question and answer section. The ISEC secretary said Mr. E.T.C "do you know the difference between aspirant and candidate?" yes my commissioner-aspirants have not been confirmed a candidate while a candidate has been confirmed vote worthy I replied- "so could you please answer the question!" I'll if it gets to me my commissioner! It's only a point off direction if you don't mind I think we are here for debate.

Though the question was not asked directly to me and answering it adds nothing to me because they were like does anybody wish to answer? No one wanted to. So I did and the students went into cheers! Hailing my name not because I was more fluent in my speeches but because I refused keep quite like all other presidential aspirants and this made them believe I would be their mouthpiece if given the opportunity.

From that point every other person within the campus saw me as the next union president; I was lifted from that stage by unknown fans, the next morning the ISEC secretary called me and here is his comment; "I need nothing from you, just go and put finishing touches to your grass root, you're the right man for the job I assure you nothing will happen to your candidacy."

And from these we became friends even as I write this work. My dear, reader, I found it difficult to delete motivational text messages I got from people after I convinced them of my sincerity of purpose and motivated them to believe in my cause. Take a look at some of it;

Don't say you shouldn't have exited without you there would be a hole in creation. A missing life to those in your family, a missing friend to those around you, A missing world.

Treasure your uniqueness it's given only to you. Play your role …

one love you have my support….anonymous fan

…good luck and all the best am behind you! Move on!!----Ag man "O" war.

… You won your opponents; you swept the crowd and convinced every one that you are the best to be MR. PRESIDENT. Manifesto day is 'ganna' be the bomb thumbs up FST is proud of you…… Caleb

…Hitler was known for his courage, king jnr. for out spookiness, JF Kennedy for boldness, Obama for his audacity and Nzeogwu for bravery, guess what E.T.C   is known for!!…… Ivor

Right now, all you need is to work on your grass root and remember there is a better word outside where nobody knows tomorrow…. Arabija PA to see secretary.

Is anybody asking you for money? …….Arabija

Good evening E.T.C is the names for candidates out just give me a call to create awareness………clement.

And a lot more of it, this brought yet the best in me; I gained more confidence on myself. I motivated so it was my turn to be motivated I believe.

IDENTIFYING

Whatever you do, wherever you are this is a very vital quality you must learn with great care.
You must be able to identify and be identified too, it as important as your life! See it that way.

Despite the fact that I have personal convictions, not minding the potentials seen within me nobody identified with me nor was my potentials identified until I personally identified my target and gave it all identity.

The presidency like I earlier said was never the target but personal integrity found in my sincerity of purpose- restoring confidence of Nigerian students to believe in the union was why I left all other post for the number one position.

Know it today that before you will be identified you must identify with people and peoples problem.

My sincerity of purpose remained elusive until I identified the problems of the union, presented feasible solutions I even went as far as identifying some rights and privileges to them. Nobody wants to follow a blind man, identified ways out for the students and in attempt of doing this I presented my real **identity** which the masses saw as worthy of note.

Do you want to aspire?
Know it that others are aspiring too!! What is that which will stand you out amongst crowd? ....That will be your weapon of victory.

Beloved am happy to tell you that once you present your true and sincere identity people must surely identify with you. Your identity can even convert your enemy to your favor. It all depends on how sincere and genuine it is. I'd a very close friend, a sister for that matter; she told me "don't go for president if you do! I'll not vote you! Go for financial secretary!!!" I ask her but why? First "you're not an indigene! Second you don't have the money!! Third you do not have looks of a president!!!" I smiled at her insults, downgrades and told her fine don't vote me since you do not have any cogent reason. People! Can you believe that this girl never talked to me until the day of the election? She was the first lady to send me a text at about 06:23:03am reads; "...success shall be yours today, wish you the best". Friends having supplied all that I have in me, after the demonstration of the will to die for my decision on my target, just at the dying minute, people began to identify with my identity hear this;

...your vote is very crucial for the way forward of Nigerian students cast wisely, vote Ezeh.t. Chinedu for proper functioning of all arms of government (legislature and judiciary)

      ....FBA president

This particular test came into my cell phone only then I knew that I have presented my identity beyond my understanding- for people to use their money to circulate this kind of message that even got to the aspirant. That was not all! There are some shocking identification, caring and sympathetic texts:-

... while congratulating you for being among the successful aspirants, I urge you to go and claim all the victory at the polls for you have what it takes to preside..........anonymous

... Today is the D-day where you will be lifted to glory. "Nigerian students are your interest, her concerns are your drive, and your competency is their motivation. You're already crowned

      .....from Paul

....good morning Mr. President, how are? Have you prayed this morning? Please if you can go to the chapel and tap blessings from the lord.......IJ

.....KOKO members are behind you the chairman (the fat guy) is behind you ride on. I'm in SMAT I assure you that Aluta number 1 is yours.

I checked in the room last night but you weren't around I checked you again in the room this morning you no day! So how far (kelechi)

… Congrats in advance God will do it for you in few hours from now. You're now our president (EZEH T CHINEDU)…… comrade prince.

…congrats, my president I don't need to tell you but it's true that U.U.K (Uzoaga) said you're good to go in IMB. Cheers!!! …….anonymous

These were some of the identifiers I was able to retain, if you have any body in FUTO as at 2010 get the rest gist from him or her. Even some believers had to believe in my identity watch this;

…… Aluta victory in JESUS NAME! Keep on moving remember be stress free so that you know the next thing to do goodnight HIS EXELLENCY!!!……… Anonymous

… I wish you success in tomorrows' election by Gods grace you are already there…. Anonymous ….please! Don't forget at a time like this consistency in humility, respect and loyalty is ABSOLUTELY important.

CONGRTULATIONS by Gods grace in advance may OUR LORD JESUS GUIDE YOU AMEN! For now, oh May God see you through SUCCESSFULLY. M.E.E my department has adopted you.

…. Call me as you receive this, to know how we can deliver you in SOSC. Hon. Ejike of IMB and NFSC final year project chairman….Anonymous

Lastly the one that beat my imagination was my off campus mike who rarely partakes in politics sending me this….

…. Congratulations our new SUG president Go!! You've made it wishing you success in your election tomorrow you are a great man by the grace of the ALMIGHT God, I'd be there to vote for you… imagine mike coming out for my cause?

NEGOTIATING

recall we said if there must be a negotiation, it must be to the favor of your decision. When all chips were down, it was obvious that I have 98% chances of making it to the presidency and to the targets, nobody wants to waste his efforts candidate who couldn't the screening, all gave me their support after we had some negotiation. Now watch this because we agreed that in the field of determination within the gate of execution you do not call for negotiation rather it will call for you, here it called for me but that does not mean you should not lobby for negotiation indirectly. It called and I lobbed it to my own greatest advantage watch this....

......PDP! Power!! You're specially invited for PDP meeting tomorrow, at 39 ......time 6:00am please be punctual (LUGARD)

This a party that had a foundation member carrying the party's flag but Mr. E.T.C was adopted in lieu of the flag bearer for reasons best known to the party's board of trustees.

.... See if you can join forces with U.U.K, Gulfment and Ikpe promising them a role in your government when you win. Do it now before Jonathan makes the move ......Arabija.

Don't forget

...negotiation and negotiating are best only when if you do not negotiate your decision will be faulty and your target missed.

Let me inform you that in all the negotiations I gained favor to my target- PDP adopted me leaving their flag bearer(conviction in bargaining) and coalition group that had earlier adopted my opponent came to the me for adoption the next morning.

In fact, all the fellow aspirant gave me their supports apart from one whom I earlier went to for negotiation and he was willing to offer me 50 000 for my precious target! I laughed at him because he failed the litmus test, I gave him.

ACHIEVING

If my target was the presidency then I can tell you that I achieved it because the entire Nigeria students came out in mass, cast their votes for me it reflected in the result as I won in majority of the departments with whooping margin and in the largest schools- SEET, SOSC and SAAT with over 1758for SEET, a 1000+ in SOSC and 21 vote difference in SAAT while the acclaimed president won mind you all the populations' put together is not up to the number of vote with which I gaped him in SOSC not to talk of SEET. In fact, record has it that his faculty is the second smallest in terms of population within the university.

How he won is what Nigerian students can't explain till date not even him can dare it. Above all, I think I achieved my set target of restoring confidence to the union electorate in believing in the union as this was seen in the reaction against some management staff refusing to pronounce me the winner.

Seeing the looming support of Nigerian students for me made sure I do not carry out that my target as their wrongs will not be spared. Since I was the people's choice and their mouthpiece, I would endanger their kleptomaniac administration. Though I didn't seat on the presidential seat, but I was a foot president.

The target was reached but never implemented, yet I was filled with joy because I stamped my identity, my foot print in the process and today am known for that identity from people comments through text messages. Read this;

…..Brother! I know they wanted to deny you, your civic right but it's too late because God of help has taken over to favor you don't be afraid because CHI GI Na EDU GI or don't you believe? It's well with you. …… Chibuike

……Brother! what is happening? I am weak, moral fiber is down, my noble appetite is at threshold, and your confessors are protesting. …EDU.

even before the result were called, I was already celebrated and when they finally released their result the above was the mood. I was not bordered for once, I waited for students' reaction with my phone off.

….good morning sir, the fact that your name is not ringing round school doesn't mean you lost. FUTO knows the truth. Keep on being the free, fair, principled and truthful man you have always been because "you are as great as the truth you tell in His PRESence" (my campaign quotes) as far as I'm concerned, you are the PRESIDENT. I respect you for being who you are don't change for anybody. …………ijeanuri.

…..how was your night my president? FUTO knows you won, and they robbed you off it continue being yourself. Have you thought of this? Without anybody's help you reached a height that others rigged to reach! God's grace in your forthcoming exams. I would have called you, but the voice is no more there but am not regretting losing it for your sake take care……..AMARA.

At this point I wish to state that of all the text I received, this once the only text that gave me hope with great synergy to forge ahead. Her text sounded as if she was in my campaign team-I saw no single help along the way financially. All those that were supposed to help were afraid that I may not be allowed to serve even if I win so no one was willing to risk money to me, I never told anyone to avoid discouraging them. How Amara got to know I don't understand but one thing I knew was that; while I was moving round with motorcycle my opponents were moving with jeep and this accorded more votes to me because they were seen as to be showing off.

Let get back to some of the text.

.... our deepest fear is not that we are inadequate, our deepest fear is that we're powerful beyond measure, so we ask ourselves "who am I to be brilliant, gorgeous, talented and fabulous?" ...actually who are you not to be? E.T.C YOU ARE A HERO, YOU'VE MADE A NAME, YOU'RE A MAN OF HONOUR....GOD BLESS YOU........ANONYMOUS

.....God knows the best for the downfall of a man is not the end of his life, therefore don't panic and don't give up for your miracle is on the way. Just calm down, and concentrate on your studies, but have this in your mind "you are born to rule not in FUTO but a place very higher than FUTO...... ANONYMOUS

.... Mistakes are painful when they happen, but years later a collection of mistakes leads us to success, be strong my brother you were the people's choice.........Chijioke

.... They have done their will which is not that of God. Every disappointment is a higher blessing to come, remember Lincoln lost all elections before winning only but the highest seat in the US, God has destined you for greater things NOT everybody has the courage to contest presidency, against Imo indigenes, I tell you one thing, I will always stand by you as far as Nigerian politics is concern and I won't forget you so soon, my brother you are a good man and continue to be good.......Adebowale Bolaji.

.... You are a man of valor I'm proud of you any day, you would go far, as far as Nigeria politics is concerned Goodluck in your exams....Jerome

.... My brother, remember life is a mixture of the *sun* (good times) and the *rain* (trying times) and the end of both is *rainbow* (your evidence) JUST HOLD ON.... I wish you success in your exams.......... Bunchy Ebere

This was a candidate I personally out pity and likeness to his undaunted spirit gave enormous support while he was contesting. He turned back act me because I was not an indigene, forgetting the fact that during his campaign he was tagged not capable in my hall I went to him, encouraged him and convinced many to listen to his plea.

Don't forget
....when injustice is done truth is inevitable.

While all these text were coming, I was thinking that people were just trying to console me; I never knew that their dashed expectation of having a mouthpiece pains them more than it pains the bearer.

Until I entered the hostel next morning and was told that the pronounced president came to my hall of residence- his phone was smashed with "a hot dirty slap" by the man o' war, according to source. He went to boys' hostels he was booed, which almost resulted in protest-fortunately for him I was there; on my appearance the entire students gave a standing ovation in a unanimous voice of Mr. president!

I thanked and urged them to pay attention to him which they did. He then pleaded I follow him to other halls though I wasn't disposed to do that. His visit to the female residents was an eye saw- as ladies poured both water and urine, chased him out of the hostel, jeering we "we do not know you, O.O (OGBE OGE) we don't know you we did not vote for you, We voted for E.T.C. even as I was told I never believed my ears until went to the hostels to say thank you to those that worked tirelessly.

It was as if they are all waiting for me to come, each hall I enter, before stepping into the door, all the residents are already out resounding applauses, and saluting my courage and unexpected victory. The ladies hostel was a show of the moment- they all came out with their cooking utensils playing songs of victory for me-what can they do? Other than grieve over their dream that has been dashed. A long awaited liberation aborted.

TERMINATING

whether Christian, Muslim or any believe, never you embark on any task without terminating plans. If you do be sure you will be terminated. Remember the world is a niche where survival of the fittest is the other of the day and that that you taste for also hungers others. Know it today that no one is interested in you rather that which is coming from you that are in you. In other to terminate it you must be prevented or face termination.

Even the Supreme Being, the almighty God, your creator make use of principles of termination. If not, why was Satan thrown down to earth? He never executed without terminating consult your holy scriptures. Also take a look at Isaiah 40:4-5 "every **valley** shall be exalted, and every *mountain* and *hills* shall be made low and the *crooked* shall be made straight and the *rough places* plain: and the *glory of the lord shall be revealed* and all flesh shall see it together: for the mouth of the lord has spoken it" that was the exact word of God, it was a revelation of his plan for future.

In it you can see zeal and assurance backed with certainty of what he said he will do and that is what he will do.

If you read carefully you will see He is more concerned with working on obstacles that will not allow the valleys to be exalted secondly His glory is not in the valley that is exalted but in doing that that made the exalted valleys visible- the lords glory is not found in his success but in the actions that lead to his success. Rigging is inevitable element in any form of election. If you don't rig, plan against rigging.

If I was to regret anything in my candidacy it will be my inability to plain for rigging or terminate rigging strategies from my opponents.

I will personally advise that once you set a target, the next should be how do I terminate close possible terminators? - Competitor. Please it must not be all negative termination, you can make close competitor weak with outstanding qualities of no measure.

◆ ◆ ◆

ILLUMINATING

Without any microcosm of doubt, I can convincingly tell you that we all are light and salt of the earth. Students of federal university of technology Owerri have for years lived in trepidation and darkness notably the nonindigenous ones.

No one could dare the cat, no one challenged the lion, and all choose to die in prejudicing. Within my spirit I was provoked, it was then I picked up the light with any atom of fear, with every step of valor.

I went into search for the truth of the matter, after which I came to a conclusion that is a true but false fact. It is a non documented reality and the same time an unfounded belief.

Beloved! Never! You allow evil to prevail around you because if it does it persists, if it persist over time it becomes a belief, if it becomes a belief, forget it surely it must become a tradition, a culture and invariably people's way of doing things.

But no matter how long it takes evil to prevail over good it must come to exposition one day. That was the case in FUTO; I had to illuminate the mind of all, convincing indigenes and non indigenes alike of the federalism of the institution. Making them understand that it has always been done like that in the past does not mean we should keep following the wrong past.

I used the weapon of the university anthem to sweep into campaign which reads…

Hurray! Our great fed-Unitech, Owerri you've come to grace, from east and west and north and south, are gathered youths of great mind and might to make Africa great….

Having shaded light to all these, the entire Nigerian students came out in mass and casted their vote for me. I can proudly tell you that *Ezeh T Chinedu* worn the 2010/2011 student union government election only the then dean of student's affair, HOD of IMT, Comr. Ibe Justine, Comr. chukwukere Levi. Comr. Anyanwu Obina and the host of other new what happened to my mandate.

To affirm what I just said about my victory in that pull, the then associate dean who letter became the dean of students affairs together with the new vice chancellor in their speeches during one of the ever recorded student crises by that hijacked administration since a decade or more state; it does not matter where you come from once you are given mandate by the students to lead them you must be allowed to serve.

And In the bid to ensuring that students choice is honored the management through the initiative of Engr. Dr. Remy Uche saw it that the election that followed the most controversial election ever in FUTO (2010/2011) was done using E-voting system for the first time in history of FUTO.

Don't forget...
Trade in that path if you must, though you may fail, but your failing may give a lot of people hope of a better tomorrow and if possible a revolution with new innovations.

If my denied mandate had been given to me maybe there would not have been any fracas in FUTO, the management won't have put much interest in the union election to talk of making it electronic voting.
By this I think my action has illuminated that aspect of FUTO because the SUG election that ensued students vote counted. And the ISEC chair man was bold enough to mount an open stand in the crowd and announce the results.

Students were jubilating on like in the past when it is always done in Dean's office and students return to their various hostel tetchy. Also, if M.K.O Abiola had not died in June 12 who knows if we would have had democracy today.
In your attempt to illuminating the world, fail if you must! Provided it is for a better tomorrow, and never! You sell the future so as not to lose out rightly; doing so makes you a myopic permanent looser.
Dear reader if you have in your plan to illuminate, also bear it in mind that you can't give what you do not have. A great knowledge

of what you are to light up must be found in you. Never have I seen any blind man leading a journey. Any mind in the prison of the world can never lead.

The world at large and our nation in particular is in dying need of a leader with a difference that person the whole Nigeria and the world at large is waiting for could be you. Illuminate yourself to be seen by the world by illuminating your immediate environment.

Beloved reader never mind that you know me, read my work as if you never knew me, for when I talk to you head to head, I speak to you like the one in the situation I mate you but when I write to you I advice you like one who has been in your shores because I do not know where you are in your current situation though I have passed it. Be assured it was these virtues that saw me through.

ORDERING FOR OPPORTUNITIES

For you to order for opportunity, you must always be at a look out while illuminating that which you wish to achieve. On no account should you be carried away by the euphoria of your illuminations I repeat. It takes a phlegmatic temperance to ink out these opportunities. Mostly occurring like an amusement.

While on my journey in the street of achievement, the opportunity presented itself for me to make a speech before the university vice chancellor and the entire students, here I had to utilize the benefits of illuminated mind by recollecting one of the quote of the great philosopher;

"with the support of we all, I doubt if anything will stop us from completing this church, because I live I doubt for doubting therefore I believe nothing is capable of stopping us from building for the Lord

not even money so I support with the sum of...to complete my three Ts- time treasure and talent"

and this earned me a general open recommendation from the vice chancellor.

He never knew I was contesting for the union presidency, immediately I dropped the microphone he ordered for it and began to rain praises on my speech saying; this is the kind of people you should have in the union, he just reminded me of my young day at UNN, this was how I use to do it and today am here.

So I urge you to put what we teach you into practice it makes us proud, in support f his donation I will double what he has given"- (10,000k) you can imagine.

Ask me what I felt like on my seat!

Already a president- I couldn't help it than to stand up and take a bow before the entire congregations, there and then I collected the confident of the catholic students and the news kept spreading the whole school, the guy is good!

Even the V.C recommended him for the union. Before that incident I have always sort for how to meet one on one with him to discuss my interest with him, in-fact I had earlier booked appointment with his PA and it failed. He then came out publicly to announce me without a cost.

Till today each time I handle microphone in the church rapt attention is often given to me to the extent that the priest called me one day and said; E.t.c! I thought your name will conk out after the election but it keeps ringing, when injustice is done truth is inevitable father I replied- well don't worry the student loves you change for nothing ok! Your time will surely come.

NECESSITATING

You may be forced to wonder, what do this gay mean? Yes I mean causing events to happen, making a need of your services to arise. Off course everyone knows and sees it as unnecessary and then? You make it a necessity. To every non-*Imolite*, it is not necessary contesting for the number one position in the university, but then why is it so? Is are they different or better candidates, or is it just a shear ethnocentrism?

For the fact that so many of the so-called indigene who occupied the office has not been able to return sanity to the system makes it a necessity for a non-indigene. This was my defense, backed up with the fact that the only non-indigenous president the union ever had left a record that has never been reached made my candidacy a necessity.

It also presented a necessity to finding why this is in vogue in a federal setting for a nation that is practicing federalism, bound in unity like Nigeria.

The evil been done to this has been exposed by the necessity my contest created, the students now knew that their mandates is purposely manipulated for selfish interests. This made them to protest when the hijacked mandate was been abused by the benefactor, be sure one thing can always lead to another.

This whole incident has drawn attention of the management to the activities of the students' union government and for the first time a leadership retreat was organized for the executives that succeeded the most openly denied mandate ever recorded in the institution.

Beloved, that was just one of my numerous trips into the journey of determination I hope I was not just entertaining your mind but activating your psyche? Did you get anything from it or are carried away?

Well which ever be the case I have not narrated this for you to praise me or show my bravery but only to convince you that until you determined you can never be that which you aspire to be.

Time and space will not permit me to tell you how I made a moneyless lady execute a project worth four hundred thousand. She had nothing in her account and so never believed anything of such could be possible but I made her to understand that; *the emptiness of the pockets is never poverty but that of the brain which has made ideas to continuously rule the world with little or no reverence to finance.*

If you do not know, know it today that; money and idea is the two undisputable commander of this world. Is either you use ideas to get money or you use money to get ideas they move along side.

You cannot get both at the same time while you are just beginning. Many fail today because they want to get money before idea no! It is ideas before money if not; you will only be a money bag and will never get power. This is one of the reasons why education remains the only source of wealth creation and the hub for national economic empowerment.

If you cannot be heard by that your next-door neighbor, there can never be a transaction between you two because she cannot hear him, and he cannot hear her. The easiest way of getting ideas is reading and reasoning. The power that everyone craves for cannot be made possible without ideas.

Dullards do not play politics if you do not know. The few one that do surround themselves with intellectuals and scholars, because they understand the rules and principle that govern success and achievements while those that thinks is all about disbursing money end up losing totally with the title 'money miss roads'.

To this end, if what is needed from you to be on hill top is determination, then learn its ways day and night I mean sleep on its arms and you will never regret you did. A daily application of what is being stated here gives you 90% assurance of success without repetitions and 147% with repetitions thanks for reading with rapt attention.

... Be determined, stay determined you will surely get there because you are on the right path of determination; be assured of a victorious exit.

ABOUT THE BOOK

This work is an undiluted self-effacing picture of determination. When the status goal is uncontrollable and unbearable, it takes one's courage and sheer determination to lead a march to the other side of the fence which is always greener. It is by determination that we discover the bright light which shines ahead of us at the other side. In darkness of termination or in determination, man is denounced deeper and deeper into the abyss of redundancy and oppression. But determination pushes him high into the aerosphere like an eagle in an aerodynamic dive to soar higher. We need to come out from our nests and fight the harsh, inhospitable ebbs of our society. The only way we can do that is by growing positive determination which EZEH T. CHINEDU has pictured well in this Dogma of determination to maintain that until you are, you can never be!!!

The author has also said that "the world is too busy to wait for you – so you better learn how to wait for the world". For a full day, listen to your language and to the language of the people around you. How often do you use and hear reactive phrases such as "if only", "I can't", or "I have to"? Anytime we think the problem is "out there" that thought is the problem, we empower what is out there to control us. The change paradigm is "outside-in" – what's out there must change before we can change. However, the proactive approach which is determination to change from inside-out: to be different, and by being different, to effect positive change in what's out there – I can be more resourceful, I can be more diligent, I can be more creative, I can be more cooperative. In the litany of determination, we discover that "to have determination is to have expected end of being at the peak." We ought to begin with the end in the mind, which is based on the principle that all things are created twice (duality of creation). There is a mental or first creation, and physical or second creation to all things. With thin in mind we could attain success which according to IBM founder T.J. Watson, "is on the far side of failure".

Therefore, in your marriage, in your studies or ventures, you should remember that people who exercise their embryonic freedom - day after day, will, little by little, expand that freedom; people who do not, will find out, that it withers until they are literally "being lived". Don't be acting out the scripts written by parents, associates, and society, instead be concerned with determination and work on being an achiever.

This book is a vade mecum, a wonderful book that could change your life. It is worth reading with profit...it is most thoughtful and enlightening. Consider the table of content and see the richness of its furniture "what does it mean to be determined?" pathway to determination, determination the only catalyst for achievement etc. all these provide a microscopic vision of determination.

Acknowledgement

With all sense of reverence and Humility, I wish to recognize the glorious and marvelous hand of God in leading me into the field of experience of all kinds. To my wonderful parents Capt.(Dr) and Mrs. A.O EZEH; brothers and sisters, siblings and relatives, friends and well-wishers, colleagues, my lord temporal and spirituals, tutors, critics and enemies; thank you all for creating a psychologically enabling environment for this work piece. To my esteemed reviewers, Prof. R.M Aguta, Dr. Jerry Obiokubuo, Rev. Fr. Dr. Lawrence O.I Iwuamadi, Seminarian Obijuru Justin C., Miss Chiamaka M. Ofoegbu, for investing your limited time in reading through this work and making an invaluable contributions in the general acceptability of this microscopic element of work, may the supreme being increase your ocean of knowledge. My utmost regard to all editors especially Dr. Ndukwe E, Yinkus Print, UI printery, all typist and iHub team that inspired this digital copy, Opera Collins, Ogechi Odekwu, Uchenna Okafor, JudeMary Onukuogu etc. Finally, to you! my beloved readers in the street of DETERMINATION, I love you all keep moving, you'll surely get there.

◆ ◆ ◆

ABOUT THE AUTHOR

Ezeh, Thomas Chinedu
is an Innovative Entrepreneur, a trained food Engineer from Enugu State, Nigeria. He is a motivational optimist, who from many leadership experiences believes that all things are possible through God who strengthens man via grace of Determination and hard work. He had his secondary Education at the famous Command Day Secondary School, Oshodi (CDSSO) where he served as the senior prefect. He Obtained  diploma in Aviation Management at Global Institute of Aviation and Maritime Technology (GIAMTECH) serving as the Deputy Governor of the set. Later proceeded to Federal University of Technology, Owerri (FUTO) where he obtained his B.Eng. Chinedu served his fathers' land at the ancient city of Ibadan (Command day School Odogbo) Under Ministry of Defence, where he taught Basic Technology. He is an alumnus of the Prestigious Lagos Business School amongst other institutions in Nigeria and Europe.

www.ingramcontent.com/pod-product-compliance
Lightning Source LLC
Chambersburg PA
CBHW031445210526
45464CB00005B/2336